Towards a New Social Work

LIBRARY OF SOCIAL WORK

GENERAL EDITOR: NOEL TIMMS

Professor of Applied Social Studies
University of Bradford

Towards a New
Social Work

edited by

Howard Jones
Professor of Social Administration,
University College, Cardiff

Routledge & Kegan Paul

London and Boston

First published in 1975
by Routledge & Kegan Paul Ltd
Broadway House, 68-74 Carter Lane,
London EC4V 5EL and
9 Park Street,
Boston, Mass. 02108, USA
Set in 10 point Pilgrim on 11 point body
and printed in Great Britain by
Northumberland Press Limited, Gateshead
ISBN 0 7100 8045 x (c)
      0 7100 8046 8 (p)

General editor's introduction

The Library of Social Work was originally designed to make a contribution to the recent significant expansion in social work education. Not only were increasing numbers of students training for social work, but the changing demands of the work and widening view of its theoretical bases were producing considerable changes in the basic curriculum of social work education. In this situation a library of short texts intended to introduce a subject, to assess its relevance for social work, and to guide further reading had a distinctive contribution to make. The continuing success of the Library of Social Work shows that this contribution is still highly valued.

A general introduction to an edited collection may seem unnecessary. Certainly one function of such general editorials in this Library – giving a brief notion of what a particular book is about – has been amply performed by Professor Howard Jones in both introduction and conclusion. It does seem appropriate, however, to say something about the place of this particular volume in the Library of Social Work.

This book is clearly not a text on a particular aspect of theory or practice; it does not expound and develop a particular theoretical perspective. It is, however, a book that concentrates on some of the central problems facing teachers, students and practitioners of contemporary social work. A high proportion of the essays are concerned with the simple but crucial question: have we got our description right? What is becoming a social worker and what is doing social work really like? Thus Mungham asks 'To what type of social formation do social workers belong?' whilst Pearson states that 'If the values of social work can be said to constitute "rules" which might act as guides to professional action, then it is clear that these rules are frequently violated and compromised and that they compete with a hidden set of rules....'

Obviously, we cannot all agree with all the questions raised in this collection and even less can we agree with the answers – if we could, it would mean social work had or posed no problems. Yet the nature of the general case for imaginative and prolonged debate in social work is established. R. G. Walton argues that the turmoil in social work generated in the 1960s can only be compared with what he describes as 'the multifarious developments in the 1860s and 1870s'.

This book makes a contribution to that debate through its wide-ranging approach and its refusal to be content with the rhetoric of polarities. So, for example, Cypher resists the view that the professional development of social work is the major and obvious obstacle to the exploration of reform concerns, and Mungham emphasises the concept of radical professionalism. Priestley alerts us to the dangers of simple solutions when he comments on the inadequacy of supposing that 'a simple awareness of the "labelling" perspective is enough to ward off the worst of its supposed consequences.' Likewise, Fowler warns of the danger that social work may become 'all things to all people, and [take] upon itself a responsibility not only for individuals, but also for the quality of the society in which we live.' The book also derives strength from the fact that most of the authors are teachers within the same School of Social Work. Schools of Social Work either as particular organisations or as clusters of organisations espousing a definite theory (as the Functional School in America) have not played a very distinctive part in the development of social work teaching. This Library could provide a means whereby more Schools in either sense could speak with a collective (but not necessarily uniform) voice.

Contents

CONTENTS

I

Introduction
Howard Jones

A process of self-searching has begun in social work. Probably as never before social workers are unsure of their professional identity : what as social workers they are aiming to do, and by what methods they might seek to achieve their aims. The bringing together in social-services departments of a polyglot collection of social workers, with very different qualifications, working with a variety of different kinds of clients, in very different administrative settings, has not, no matter how desirable it might be on other grounds, helped the profession to find itself. The present addition to this 'general' service, of social workers in hospital and psychiatric medicine, together with the changes contingent on the reform of local government, can only serve to prolong the present confusion.

For confusion it is. At one end one has those social workers (and course tutors) who still see the future in terms of an élite of casework technologists delicately utilising the nuances of personal relationship as a means towards enabling their clients to live more successfully within a world which is seen as largely outside their control or the control of their caseworkers. At the other end are the younger and more radical spirits within the profession for whom this is an arid creed.

Nobody would suggest that the radical movement in social work arose in isolation from more general currents of opinion in society at large. We see a general swell of feeling, particularly among the young towards taking a greater share in determining their own destiny, and using the power thus claimed to remedy what they feel to be social injustice. And this new confidence in their power to shape events has spread even to groups who, for a long time, had been believed not only to have no right to intervene, but no capacity for doing so—such as the clients of the public welfare services and inmates of our penal institutions. The emergence of bodies like the Claimants Union, and PROP (Preservation of the

Rights of Prisoners) has effectively given the lie to these assumptions. Many social workers have been involved in these movements; and with the emergence of a single professional body, the British Association of Social Workers (BASW), from the various specialised associations, they began, as they saw it, to try to 'set their own house in order'.

Since then the debate in BASW has waxed fierce and long. And on the extreme left of the profession, has emerged an organisation called Case-Con—a cynical abbreviation of the words case conference in such a way as to imply that this time-honoured institution of social casework, ostensibly intended to bring the collective wisdom of a group of social workers to bear upon a particular case, was in fact a confidence trick perpetrated by the social workers on their clients.

The emergence of community work as a social work technique merely exacerbated these difficulties by bringing into the open the basic incompatibility within social work which lies behind them. On the one hand there is the 'social adjustment' objective sought by public authorities through the agency of the social workers they employ for that purpose. In opposition to this is the traditional 'client orientation' of social casework, continued also in community work. This lays stress upon the client's ultimate right, after having been helped by the social worker to understand his situation, of deciding himself what to do about it.

There were bound to be conflicts between social workers, and their employers in such circumstances. So we got social workers being dismissed, because they had embarrassed the local authorities who employed them by encouraging (or at least not discouraging) the local communities with whom they were working to resist actions of the local authority which they felt to be wrong or unfair. Social workers demonstrated outside their own town halls. Ministers of the Crown responsible for parts of the welfare state received hostile receptions at meetings of BASW. And in schools of social work, students found themselves being taught by tutors whose views were diametrically opposed to one another.

All of which may at first sight seem to present a rather depressing prospect. To the various contributors to this book, it is however, nothing of the kind. The old unsatisfactory mould has been broken, and it has become possible at last to look at the basic issues in social work without preconceptions, for the first time since the war. The ideas being debated are not very new; the social reform perspective which is being presented as the main counter to psycho-dynamically oriented casework was, as Mr Cypher points out in his contribution to this book, an important part of early social work. But that perspective is being revived in entirely new circumstances. We do now have a highly skilled body of caseworkers who represent not only a powerful vested interest and a persuasive body of theory, but also have a long history of indisputable service to their clients and to the community. And on the other side we have much interest among social workers in that developing body of theory from sociology which shows that our social problems often arise more from structural features of our society than from personal problems within individuals.

It is time for the fighting to stop and the debate to start. It is to initiate a debate on some of these issues that the authors of the following papers came together. All except two are teachers within the School of Social Work at University College, Cardiff, the exceptions being individuals who share ideas and personal friendship with some of the others. So in effect this is a contribution to the debate from the School of Social Work, at University College, Cardiff, and we claim no monopoly of wisdom or even total agreement between ourselves. We invite you to join in and takes sides.

2

Social reform and the social work profession: what hope for a 'rapprochement?'
J. R. Cypher

In looking at the genesis of social work in nineteenth-century Britain, it has been viewed as a 'social movement' concerned through 'disciplined and principled forms of social action to find more realistic remedies to social problems'.[1] With the advent of salaried and trained social workers, the beginning of the process of professionalization, a new social work emerged, with change in form and content, and a consequent shedding of its 'movement' qualities. This has continued until today when, as a result of criticism from without and within, professional social work[2] has begun to appraise the nature of its response to contemporary conditions. To some extent it can be argued, and this will be a concern of this essay, that professional social work is returning to its origins in social reform. How complete this *rapprochement* can be is problematic. There are formidable obstacles—professional developments, the bureaucratization of service and even some of the characteristics of those who form the bulk of today's professional social work force. These obstacles will be examined in some detail to enable us to gauge the potential for an explicit commitment by professional social work to social reform. It is our contention that the presence or absence of a reformist commitment amongst social work personnel cannot be explained solely by reference to an analysis of the professional elements in social work but must include consideration of the work-place and the non-work situation of social workers.

At its simplest, a social movement has been viewed as a series of actions and endeavours of a body of persons for a special object,[3] but this concept has been subject to much 'refinement' by political scientists and others. From the diversity of conceptualizations a working concept has been distilled which captures the essential characteristics of social movement.[4] These are, in an abridged form:

4

1 A deliberate and collective endeavour to promote change in any direction and by any means. (A movement may be inspired by the pursuit of, for example, proletarian or fascist objectives and employ violence or extra-legal methods to obtain its ends.)

2 A minimal degree of organization.

3 Support for change based on normative commitment to the movement's aims of, and active participation by, the members.

The social work of the late nineteenth century did at a minimum level evidence these movement characteristics.[5] There was a strong normative commitment to the alleviation of social problems and reduction of conflict in society. This was promoted in a variety of ways through such forms as the university settlements, contacts with government that influential élites enjoyed, tenants' associations and charity visiting. Certainly any real organizational cohesion in social work was lacking at that time, and it is ironical that closer association between groupings came with the concern to provide training, an event which contributed to the growth of professional social work and the decline of social work as a social movement. This had not been a movement concerned to redistribute power in favour of underprivileged groups, and for many of the participants their own superior economic status was assured. Instead, as Sherwell observes, 'the social worker holds a brief not for a class but for a principle of justice and right dealing'.[6]

Notwithstanding certain ideological differences within the social work movement particularly between the Charity Organisation Society and the settlements, social work as a movement consolidated its position in the early years of the twentieth century. As late as 1920 in his book *The Social Worker* Attlee noted 'the demand of the social reformer today is for a new attitude to social problems rather than for specific reform in any department of life.... Every social worker is almost certain to be also an agitator.'[7] If by the term 'social worker' Attlee included the trained and untrained person, the volunteer and the salaried, all with a part to play in furthering general social reform, he was speaking of a social work which was already changing with the beginnings of professional social work and the fall of the volunteer already underway. Almoners (now medical social workers) had been in post since 1895. The proximity of other professional workers in the hospital setting and the exposure to medical concepts and treatment regimes influenced these forerunners of the professional social worker. With the advent of the probation officer, a process was begun whereby the new professional social work gradually became fragmented into specialist practice areas associated with particular organizational settings.

It would be erroneous to conclude that the inter-war years in this country were a time of complete divorce between social work as a professional occupation and as a social movement. Settlements and volunteer activities were still alive—unemployment and its attendant evils were a new rallying point—but professional social work with a new emphasis on the 'relationship' with the individual client was focusing on personality rather than society. The 'psychiatric deluge' well describes events in America at this time but professional social work in Britain, mainly existing in medical and psychiatric spheres, was at a less developed stage and the effect on British social work practice, though real, was less dramatic. Primarily a means for developing the common elements in professional social work and including amongst the constituent organizations an independent group of psychiatric social workers stressing the importance of emotional problems, the establishment of the British Federation of Social Workers in 1935 illustrates, nevertheless, the continuing link between embryonic professional social work and the wider social work movement; Lees argues that concern with social policy underlay much of the activities of the Federation in the 1930s.[8]

The often uncritical acceptance of Freudian concepts and treatment modes by professional social workers has been variously interpreted. It may be viewed as the end of the search for a knowledge base on which the claim to professional status could be based. Here the focus on the individual, and intra-psychic affairs, offered an opportunity for professionals to claim a special sphere of operations in comparison with the wider area of social reform where professional social work could hardly claim a monopoly. An alternative and plausible explanation in examining the decline of the movement dimension in social work, and one employing a sociopolitical perspective, is offered by Bitensky.[9] Looking at the American scene and the success of social workers such as Jane Adams and Grace Abbot in achieving legislative reforms that changed the social order, he suggests that these successes particularly in the development of 'new deal' governmental provision, invalidated the credentials of a social work oriented to a social reform perspective. With the achievement of these real reforms, social work's *raison d'être* was no more. The problem posed did not end there, for, given that social work was primarily located in private agencies, reconsideration of its position *vis-à-vis* new governmental agencies was required. Freudian psychology on this view offered an opportunity not so much to promote the professional status of social work, but rather to support its continuing existence by providing a new and relevant rationale. From that point in time, circa the 1930s, social work, or now more correctly

social casework as it had become, 'embarked on the road of dedica-
tion to intensive psychotherapy that has not changed until recent
times'.[10]

It is necessary to move Bitensky's analysis forward in time to
make it applicable to British professional social workers. With the
post-Second World War reforms in this country and the creation
of an elaborate and encompassing range of social services, there
was widespread belief that poverty, illiteracy and ill-health would
be effectively tackled. As Titmuss[11] has observed, there were even
those who prophesied the demise of the welfare state, made
irrelevant by the Age of Affluence brought in on the twin horses
of full employment and increased equality of opportunity. Social
workers, too, accepted that social ills were largely being remedied.
Did not Seebohm Rowntree's final York study give empirical support for such a view?[12] Within this overall context a shift by
social work services to the individual and his psychic environment
seemed especially germane. Further, with the many services
provided statutorily and the post-war reform spirit conveying a
new relationship between state and citizen, social work as a social
movement seemed to have achieved its objects. Voluntarism still
persisted; the existence of state provision did not lead to the atrophy
of voluntary action as had been feared, but there was a marked
alignment with state schemes. Voluntary associations adopted contributory and complementary roles with a consequential reduction
in their contributions as pioneers of social reform or citadels of
challenge.

The rediscovery of poverty by researchers at the London School
of Economics in the early 1960s marked the beginning of the end
of satisfaction with (or complacency about) the welfare state.[13]
Evidence of the large numbers of people living below the Government's own minimum living standard,[14] reports pointing to the
wastage of ability amongst young people at all education levels,[15]
the housing crisis of the early 1960s, and dissatisfaction with the
administrative divisions between the social services and the lack of
mutual reinforcement of their efforts[16] were all events forcing
reappraisal. The role of social work as a social movement and the
rise and 'fall' of the welfare state has been succinctly described by
Perlman and Gurin. They note the paradox in social reform:[17]

It usually springs from passionate indignation but has a way
of setting like plaster into institutional moulds. The end
result ... may well be an efficiently operating bureaucracy
engaged in doing what the reformer had worked so hard
to bring into existence, but the outcome often seems alien to
the reformer who started the process. The programme

7

that emerges becomes either flaccid or rigid, and a new
cycle of discontent and reform is generated.

Today, the new cycle of reform is to be found prompted by such
groups as Shelter, The Child Poverty Action Group (CPAG) and a
whole host of client and community groups. Social workers as
radical individuals are often involved with these groups in calling
for reforms but the emergence of a radical social work profession
has been delayed. Critics point to the obsession of professional
social workers with professional issues—the development of casework theory, practice skills and the admission and control of the
novice. If the alignment with Freudian psychology and methods
was, as Bitensky suggests, functional for the very existence of social
work at the time of developing and universal state welfare programmes, the continual focus on individual personality when the
wider social service complex was found to be so seriously wanting,
now seemed related to the narrow professional claims and desires
of trained social work practitioners. In the late 1960s these social
workers became organized not to secure social reform but rather
to further their own professional interests. Lobbying, working
parties and the writings of social workers were concentrated on the
formation of a unified social work association and to secure the
implementation of the Seebohm Report. One commentator noted
that 'both in doing and teaching, the scene in social work is
parochial and safe'.[18] No doubt some social workers were surprised
that the Chairman of the Seebohm Committee that had argued so
forcefully for changes that would promote social work as a professional occupation and enhance career prospects, should nevertheless observe that it is poverty and bad housing which 'probably
cause something like 60% of the work that is now carried on by
social workers'.[19] But the question of whether expenditure on other
social services might be increased by a reappraisal of the investment
in social work never became a significant debating point within
social work and its association, the British Association of Social
Workers (BASW).

This is not to say that the profession, through its Association,
is failing to engage in some reappraisal. There are some professional
workers who are aware of the role that what is viewed as 'good
casework practice' plays in distracting attention from the structural
ills in society. Increasingly professional journals have contained
articles on reform strategies and radical tactics in social work.[20]
Conferences have been held to examine objectives and practice,
particularly in relation to community work. BASW has established
a social action working party[21] and recently in an attempt to revive
flagging interest at BASW branch level both as a counter-measure

and as an acknowledgment of the growing concern of some social workers about these matters, the chairman of the Association has called for branches to engage in reform activities in the local government arena.[22] But what impact do such exhortations have on the average professional social worker? Does he shed his individualistic orientation and disengage himself from the prescription for inactivity suggested by such precepts as self-determination and acceptance which form the profession's ethical code, in favour of intellectual and emotional alignment with the client, and ultimately joint action to resolve the structural dysfunctions in society?

It should be remembered that social work as an occupation is differentiated in many ways—agency setting, client group, skill levels, length of training—yet this does not always prevent the use by its critics of rather unrealistic stereotypes, these being rather encouraged by the lack of serious factual investigation. In particular there are few British studies which examine professional social workers' orientations with regard to what is, for convenience, called the social reform/individual adjustment dilemma. Lees[23] has argued that in a BASW branch he studied, there was considerable sympathy for social reform objectives and this is echoed in a pilot study undertaken by the present writer.[24] Admittedly these studies do refer only to those who are in membership of BASW, an association of approximately half of the 19,513 people who work in designated social work posts in the public sector.[25]

Even so, it is difficult when viewing professional social work at this time as it is practised, to agree wholeheartedly that social work is 'an open system of ideas . . . and it has no inherent commitment to viewing the world as flat'.[26] Meyer contends that its greatest viability lies in its ability to accommodate to changing perceptions. Professional concerns and preoccupations may be too well established for any major accommodation to changing perceptions. This is not to deny that within the professional association there is a group of members subscribing to reform ideals. It is around this group that the movement qualities of social work might grow amongst professionals. This in turn could lead to a stronger alignment with the variety of bodies ranging from university settlements to Shelter that are external to professional social work and have kept alive the movement dimension.

The implementation of the Seebohm recommendations may contribute to an enlargement of this group. The incorporation of generic practice in Social Services departments offers opportunities for workers to develop interests in a wide range of clients. Further, in the larger of these departments the worker will often play an administrative role in deciding how resources are to be utilized. Rationing becomes his responsibility and he may become more aware of choices and shortages. This experience may be such as to force more social workers to snap out of a concern with means (methods) and focus on values, choices and reform concerns. The seeds of a *rapprochement* in which professionals participate in the wider social work movement are present, but the profession seems patently ambivalent showing both defensiveness and receptivity to change. The obstacles are formidable and the radicals in the profession are few.

Contrary to the usual view, we do not regard the professional development of social work as the major or obvious obstacle. The professionalization process does not inevitably lead to a weakening of the 'social' in social work. Epstein has distinguished between structural and ideological aspects in the professionalization process.[27] His empirical study suggests these two elements need to be considered separately. He finds no evidence to suggest that professional social workers are members of a structurally integrated community, rather there is a hierarchy of normative commitments extending from agency to professional association. Conservatism appears related solely to the possession of a professional ideology which prescribes the nature of contact with clients and de-emphasizes intimacy. Meyer too observes how professional social work has developed as if it were a 'modified form of psycho-analytical practice requiring a maximum of social distance between worker and client'.[28] But even so there is nothing to suggest that a uniform and conservatizing professional ideology is transmitted—the very diversity amongst schools of social work staff members concerning practice and models of change must operate against the transmission of a uniform ideology—to say nothing about variation in student receptivity in the teaching situation.[29] More-over, Bucher and Strauss have advocated that a process approach to the study of professions provides a more realistic statement of their functioning.[30] This recognizes that notions of unity or com-munity are a smoke-screen for public relations purposes, a veneer which if removed will reveal warring segments within professions.

Certainly in the case of BASW, community characteristics have not notably been to the fore. The meetings of constituent organiza-tions of social workers that merged to form BASW acknowledged the existence of a common core of values and practices that would unify social work but this oft-mentioned unity seems as yet, unrealized. Of course, the Standing Conference of Organizations of Social Workers was committed to change and may have sought common principles where none existed. Rein, surveying American social work, concludes that the search for a single common pro-fessional creed is illusory: 'there are many creeds and many belief systems.'[31] The recent altercation within BASW over the employment of health service social workers by local authority social services departments resulting in innumerable constitutional wrangles and strife within and between the sections of BASW is illustrative of this.[32] Support for a change in the employment situation of health service social workers came from Section Three of the Association and it is within this section that (generalizing from the present writer's pilot study) a reform zeal is to be found, with Section Two showing an even more pronounced radical presence as can be seen in table 2·1.[33]

TABLE 2·1   *Ideologies of change* (N=62)

Sections	Favouring individual adjustment (%)	Favouring social change (%)	No answer (%)
1 Physical Illness and Handicap	40	30	30
2 Mental Health	25	69	6
3 Child and Family Social Work	46	43	11
4 Treatment of Offenders	67	33	0

Epstein has constructed an Index of Commitment to Activist Goals based on a typology formed from the combination of responses to questionnaire items dealing with the objectives of social work intervention and the intended recipients of service.[34] With slight modifications this was incorporated in the pilot study, those questioned being invited to identify their position with regard to the individual adjustment/social reform dichotomy and give their views on the community-wide provision of social work services or selective provision in favour of the disadvantaged. This latter concern clearly has salience at the level of delivery of service for American workers where private agencies have some choice in the clientele they serve and where in the public sector there is not the same comprehensive service as exists in Great Britain. The British workers may have viewed this questionnaire item as related to ideology, with in some cases the answers indicating a preference for a method of delivery of service which it might not be possible to operate in this country. The findings are shown in table 2·2 and discussed below.

TABLE 2·2 *Goal orientation of respondents by sectional membership**

Sections	Therapists (%)	Traditionalists (%)	Reformists (%)	Activists (%)
1	40	0	30	0
2	25	0	44	25
3	39	7	18	25
4	33	17	33	0
All Sections	47	7	28	18

* Not all respondents were classifiable.

'Therapists' describes those workers viewing individual adjustment as the object of their professional intervention and who believe that service should be provided for all social groups in the community. Referring to the sectional membership of the respondents the therapist orientation is one which is grounded in all fields of social work practice, although mental health workers and those with interest in mental health (section 2) seem less inclined to this orientation. 'Traditionalists' refers to those working to achieve individual adjustment yet with a preference for concentrating their service on the disadvantaged. Within this small group who seemingly want to adopt a 'hard-line' approach to certain clients, probation officers (section 4) appear to the fore with section 1 (mainly medical social workers) and section 2 respondents completely absent.

'Reformists' describes those who favour some change in the social environment as the object of their work with clients, without restricting the service only to the disadvantaged. Again all fields of social work contain certain workers with this orientation, it being most strongly evidenced by those in the mental health field. Is this a reflection of their belief in the significance of social factors in the causation of mental illness, a problem which many see as affecting all social groups in the community? Similarly concerned to achieve social reform and change in their professional intervention are those designated 'activists'. However, their preference is for concentrating social work effort on the disadvantaged. It is suggested that these are all the allies of the poor, striving to secure improvement in the latter's overall socio-economic status. Certain workers with backgrounds in mental health and child care are the only ones found here who seem to favour not therapy nor adjustment, but the concentrated effort to secure change. It remains to be determined whether their orientation is a product of ideological commitment, experience of working with the disadvantaged or a combination of these (and other) factors.

There may be a little ambiguity in the category of activists. Some of them may indeed be concerned with remedying inequalities, while others who have the same objectives may nevertheless reject the concentration of service on the have-nots which defines this group because of the stigmatizing, means-testing association of 'selective provision'. Nevertheless, the activists were, at a statistically significant level, more likely to have taken part in demonstrations. And while 'non-activists' favoured aims for the professional association like 'furthering the advance of social work as a profession' or, 'fostering public knowledge about social work', activists urged as a primary aim that BASW should 'take such steps as are necessary to promote *directly* the welfare of individuals and community social well-being'. Clearly we have here a group with a genuine radical orientation properly described as activists. Respondents were also invited to identify the things they regarded as most important to them in their work. For some, the answer was 'a high degree of freedom whilst at work', and many regarded as most important 'opportunities to provide maximum services to clients'. However, activists differed in the importance they attached to recognition from colleagues in the profession.

Taking these findings together there is a suggestion that activists view the professional association as a vehicle for the expression of radical concerns, and seek recognition from members sharing those concerns. Thus we find within BASW some professional workers who are keen to further the movement element but many are not, seemingly wishing instead to continue with their familiar and established goals and skills (see table 2·1). We turn now to look at organizational and non-work factors that may explain some of this.

It might be expected that, whatever the pros and cons of the professional process in social work, it serves to protect the client from the dictates of bureaucracy with the professional worker standing between client and agency. In looking at some of the evidence on the attitudes and behaviour of social workers, Rein argues that 'they reveal the extent to which social workers personally comply with bureaucratic norms even when these conflict with client needs'.[35] As recently as 1965, a study of social workers in a British local authority's social work departments showed the limited professional development of staff and the notable absence of workers sharing in policy-making.[36] The study concludes that the situation of social workers in local government 'shows them to be in a rather uncomfortable position. Yet the majority were satisfied with their work.'

The recent expansion of training courses has no doubt increased the proportion of professional social work staff in local government, but even where professional workers are to the fore it has been found that, in spite of the social worker's intellectual and emotional commitment to meeting the needs of his client, compliance with agency rules was 'the rule' when these were in conflict with the worker's own estimation of the needs of clients.[37] Studies of social work students which might show them as bringing radicalism wholesale into social work practice should be received with caution. Recent American research suggests that a noticeable commitment to innovation by students in training, gives way, when they are established in practice, to support for the *status quo*.[38]

Social work as an occupation often appears in a historical perspective to be more bureaucratized than professionalized. Rea Price for instance notes the special circumstances which gave rise to Children's Departments; the Dennis O'Neil scandal and hierarchical structures that developed to strengthen supervision and prevent the recurrence of such events.[39] Professional norms and practices are being gradually superimposed especially in recent years, on an extant bureaucratic structure, but social work remains best-characterized as a semi-profession because of the theoretical weakness of its knowledge base and short training period. As such it tends toward heteronomy, workers being subject to direction by administrative superiors and rules of the organization; this as opposed to autonomy where the norms governing behaviour are a product from within the professional group.

Whatever professional social work may claim as the virtues for casework practice of supervision in social work agencies, it should be recognized that it serves as a device to facilitate not merely behavioural but attitudinal conformity to agency policies and practice by workers whose contact with clients cannot in the nature of things be more directly controlled. In his study of County Agency, a public welfare department with a casework staff totalling 104, Scott refers to the supervisor's sleight of hand which 'identified an essentially bureaucratic trait—the ability to accept authority—as a professional characteristic'.[40] One's level of maturity was indicated by one's disciplined conformity to authority. Scott shows, by reference to the social work literature, that challenge to the agency ('immaturity') is seen as a feature of student social workers. The ultimate aim of tutors and field supervisors is to promote his 'maturity'. In this way, the social worker's potential for challenging agency policy is cooled out. There is evidence to suggest that social work supervisors exhibit a greater bureaucratic orientation than do basic grade workers.[41] If these American findings relating to contacts between professionals in the agency apply to Britain, and are added to the traditional British public sector emphasis on loyal service, we should not expect large members of social workers to adopt critical or 'change' stances. Sytz has portrayed graphically the essence of the agency/worker relationship when he talks of the re-enactment of 'The Charge of the Light Brigade'—' "Theirs not to make reply, theirs not to reason why, theirs but to do and die" only of course, they do not die, they either leave the profession or linger on until they thoroughly learn the ritual of "acceptance of agency", "acceptance of supervision".'[42]

The present writer's pilot study suggests that it is within sections 2 (Mental Health) and 3 (Child and Family Social Work) of BASW that those with an activist orientation are located. Given that these people and the 'non-activists' work within the bureaucratic framework of the local government service some explanation is called for. Necessarily in view of the small number of activists in our sample, the suggested explanation is to be regarded as tentative. It centres on an examination of the biographical data of these social workers, in particular social class origins and educational experiences.

We shall cite a number of personal characteristics of social workers which could explain the lack of a pronounced reform commitment in the profession or challenge to agency policies. Being female and without experience of higher education and coming from an upper working-class background, are common features of professional social workers. But we have noted the presence of activists and it is of interest that in certain respects, their personal characteristics do differ from other social workers.

Unlike those early social workers who were part of the movement era with its social reform objectives, today's professional social workers have experienced a theory and practice directed towards the individual. And an individual moreover who is demonstrating some personal malfunction within a society where there exists a comprehensive range of social services. In social work education even now, the primary feature of social work (casework) that is stressed to new recruits is that of providing direct service to clients through a relationship. This must seem particularly relevant to many women as an occupation which seems to offer such opportunities for expressing the care and nurturant elements of the female role. This is not necessarily to support the view that women's biology totally governs their destiny, neither is it accepted that all that is subsumed under the masculinity/femininity distinction is a product of culture.

Since it is women who produce the babies and are substantially concerned with their care and upbringing, by extension (and here cultural factors are influential) we give to women many of the nurturant tasks that society requires carried out for the aged, weak and infirm. But to talk of tasks determined by culturally assigned sex status may be insufficient; sexuality is more pervasive. New contraceptive aids and changing mores may alter our view of the tasks traditionally related to women through their reproductive capacity, but these do not necessarily affect women's sexuality. Sexuality makes men and women in Ruderman's words 'in their nature, in their very being, unlike yet unalike—to some small but critical degree, essentially, qualitatively, different'.[43] Following from this some psychologists contend that female sexuality or femininity means that when compared with men, women are 'generally more nurturant, dependent, passive, receptive, maternal, intuitive, emphatic and labile and that these characteristics become stronger as girls become women'.[44]

When women enter the work-place they are attracted to those occupations like social work that emphasize interpersonal communication, empathy, subjectivity and nurturance. Such occupations are traditionally filled by women because of the personal qualities, derived from femininity and reinforced by socialization, that women possess. Tables 2·3a and 2·3b show the preponderance of females over males in and about to enter the social work profession. It would seem to follow that for the many social workers who are women giving service directly to individuals and being submissive to the authority of the agency will be acceptable features of the job. Such people do not necessarily enter social work filled with a zeal for reform and neither does the agency encourage them to develop any such zeal that may be latent.

TABLE 2·3a *Percentage of social workers by sex as reported in several studies*

Study	Male (%)	Female (%)	No. in study
1 Parker and Allen	39	61	70
2 Nursten *et al.*	43	57	110
3 Cypher	40	60	65

1 J. Parker and R. Allen. See note 36.
2 P. Nursten, *et al.*, *Social Workers and their Clients*, Research Publication Services, 1972.
3 J. Cypher. See note 24.

TABLE 2·3b *Percentage of American social work students by sex and by social work method**

	Total (%)	Casework (%)	Groupwork (%)	Community Organization (%)
Male	40·8	36·3	47·0	56·3
Female	59·2	63·7	53·0	43·7

* D. Golden, *et al.*, *Students in Schools of Social Work*, Council on Social Work Education, 1972.

To the extent that the occupation undergoes change such as the call for a reform commitment and use of militant or conflict-laden approaches, women's passivity and nurturance may be less relevant. They may even resist such developments or leave them to men and to women with the requisite masculine traits. In this respect the larger number of male students specializing in community organization as a social work method as shown in table 2·3b is of interest. Bardwick argues that the visibility of the personality qualities of femininity is determined by role in addition to individual personality traits.[45] If some women are able to bring masculine personality characteristics to social work and be successful, this may explain the presence in the history of social work of many examples of female social reformers such as the Americans mentioned earlier.

Inspection of the activists in our own study shows that women are represented (15 per cent) but there are nearly twice as many men (27 per cent). The drive, assertion and commitment necessary for direct action are not generally features of women, hence perhaps their small share of this group. However, as the above figures show, only a minority of men, although a large minority, are committed to the direct action stance.

Social work as an activity has long been associated with the upper and middle classes. The swish of Lady Bountiful's skirts as she went about her visiting has continued to be heard long after her departure from the social work scene. As social work became institutionalized in modern industrial societies with public and large-scale private agencies organizing for service, the increase in the number of social work posts has offered opportunities to greater numbers of people from different social class backgrounds. New work developments have gone on in concert with such factors as changes in the structure of the family, education and migration and others which affect this process of widening opportunities.

Historically the professions have long offered opportunities to able lower-class persons to enhance their social positions.[46] Today in our more open society semi-professional occupations like nursing and social work, each with their own educational facilities for equipping the recruit, are furthering the process of extending opportunities to lower-class individuals. Whether it is the image of social work as a middle-class occupation or the status of a public official, most common in this country, which serves to heighten the attractiveness of social work is difficult to determine. This is not meant to imply that social work is now mainly staffed by recruits from lower-class backgrounds; available evidence shows no distinct pattern. But it is clear that increasingly for many people it does facilitate upward movement.

Surveying American studies which explore the social-class origins of semi-professionals, Simpson and Simpson show how inconclusive are the findings.[47] British evidence is sparse but the contents of table 2·4 mirror the American results. In this table the social-class backgrounds by reference to fathers' occupations of social workers featuring in two recent studies are presented. Nursten, studying social workers employed in a town in the North of England, found that a substantial majority came from white-collar backgrounds. The present writer's findings from a sample of professionally qualified workers drawn from industrial South Wales shows a greater spread with a larger proportion of workers coming from blue-collar backgrounds. Here there is a suggestion of some workers having experienced upward mobility.

Upward social mobility can be viewed as the achievement by an individual of an occupation more highly evaluated than that obtained by his father. For many individuals this movement will entail a change in orientation from the class they are leaving toward the one they aspire to join. Anticipatory socialization, the adoption of the values of a group or stratum to which an individual aspires but does not belong, serves according to Merton 'the twin functions of aiding his rise into that group and of easing his adjustment after he has become part of it'.[48] Within a relatively open society such as ours, there is limited provision for social mobility facilitated particularly by the wide range of tasks required to be carried out and the availability of educational facilities to prepare new and existing members of the work force. In many instances anticipatory socialization will be followed by the gaining of higher social status. Although this may be functional for the individual, it poses a threat to the class being supplanted. As Merton observes: 'Allegiance to the contrasting mores of another group means defection from the mores of the in-group.'[49] Applying this to upwardly mobile social workers it would be surprising to find such people retaining a strong identification with the working class and a commitment to social reform to improve the position of that class. Jackson and Marsden[50] have identified the role of the grammar school as an agent in contributing to a change in reference group orientation and in preparation for upward mobility, and as a minimum many social workers have obtained a grammar school education. In the writer's study it was found that the modal social-class background of non-activists by reference to their fathers' occupation was 5b, a lower-class position. In contrast the activists' modal score on class origins was 3, a middle-class position. We shall return to this finding later in the discussion of the activists and their correspondence to the role of intellectual.

TABLE 2·4 *Social class origins of certain social workers by reference to fathers' occupation*

Study	Registrar General's classification of occupation					
	1	2	3	4	5	Unclassified
1 Nursten *et al.* (%)	7	31	52	6	3	2

	Hall-Jones scale of occupational prestige								
	1	2	3	4	5a	5b	6	7	Unclassified
2 Cypher (%)	5	12	25	9	5	26	6	2	10

1 P. Nursten *et al.* as in table 2·3a.
2 J. Cypher. See note 24.

Research on the process of ageing suggest that, in general, it is older people who are more rigid in their attitudes and behaviour than younger people and the former are also less likely to adapt to changing stimuli. Concerning political ideology, conservative stances tend to be more widespread amongst older age groups as is shown in their greater resistance to change and lesser tolerance, even when educational background is controlled, of political and social deviants.[51] In his study of English social workers Lees found when analysing his sample by age that 'the older groups tended to be less "extreme" in attitude'.[52] In our study support for reform is spread throughout the age-range but as with Lees, greater support for conflict as opposed to consensus strategies of change is located amongst younger social workers. Given our limited knowledge we can only speculate on the reasons for differences by age.

For the middle-aged social worker support for the direct promotion of change may be too disruptive to his psychological and social well-being or, as Schein suggests, 'his cautiousness or his restraint may have adaptive value for his daily life as he confronts alterations in his health or his social environment'.[53] We do not know if in the case of older social workers their personalities have been changed through ageing and if they have, whether these changes are products of events in the social environment or individual physiology. In social work many of the younger entrants to the profession have an educational background superior to that of older, established colleagues. Age differences regarding methods of change as well as other features of social work theory and practice may be a consequence of differential educational experiences. (The impact of education on different age cohorts is of course a matter of wider importance in examining 'generation gaps'.) Our findings and those of Lees might be seen as giving some support to the view that social workers and other people possess a 'fixed educational background that functions sociologically in almost the same way as such inborn characteristics as skin colour or sex'.[54]

There is no support for the proposition that activists are especially mobile in their careers. Sixty-one per cent of them have worked in their present agencies for 4 years or more, with the average period of employment in the present agency being 3·8 years for activists compared with 4·0 years for non-activists. Moreover, experience of social work practice is not brief amongst activists; the median of 7·3 years compares not too unfavourably with that of 8·2 years for non-activists The activists then are not exclusively young idealists recently recruited to social work. It is of interest also that for some workers with a lengthy agency experience their radicalism has not been cooled out.

If social work has a stronger emotional rather than intellectual appeal we might expect to find this reflected in the educational patterns of workers.[55] Some allowance will have to be made for the earlier restricted opportunities for higher education, particularly for women. However, for many workers, the grammar school is the end of their formal education. Others have taken professional courses but until very recently, as shown in table 2·5, it is only a small minority who have a university degree in addition to professional training.

TABLE 2·5   *Qualifications of social workers as reported in several studies*

Study and year of data collection	Degree and social work qualification (%)	Social work qualification (%)	Other qualifications or none (%)
1 Parker and Allen (1965)	10	13	77
2 Cypher (1971)	32	68	0

1 J. Parker and R. Allen. See note 36.
2 J. Cypher. See note 24.

This leads to a major point of distinction, namely that activists are, at a statistically significant level ($\chi^2 = 4·79$, $\rho < 0·05$), more likely to have read for a social science degree prior to commencing professional training. Other studies document a strong tendency for middle-class persons who have experienced higher education to vote for leftist parties.[56] These provide support for the proposition that higher education does have a radicalizing effect on those who experience it. Grammar school education contributes to the inculcation of middle-class norms and values. In comparison 'higher education—particularly at University—can be conceived of, in part at least, as a "de-socialization" process insofar as it inculcates a questioning and critical attitude to certain values'.[57] Parkin's work on the membership of CND, another example of a social movement, brings out the strong support for and participation in its activities by sociology students.

It is plausible that social science graduates who enter social work are as much interested in intellectual concerns as with matters of the heart; an intellectual concern which has alerted them to the discrepancy between notions of democracy, equality and freedom and the social situation. Through what has been called the 'priestly mode' the social work tutor is said to indoctrinate, then examine and finally ordain the recruit.[58] It remains the subject of debate whether such a deradicalizing process takes place in any uniform or widespread sense given that many social work courses are staffed by tutors with often conflicting ideologies on professional issues. However, social science graduates might be better insulated from any deradicalizing effects of both the professional training and agency procedures and look to the professional association and other outlets forming part of the wider social work movement to pursue reform objectives.

If we combine the tentative findings from our study, we obtain a profile of the social work activist. In general such a worker is male (or female with masculine traits), of middle-class origin, possesses a university social science degree and is somewhat younger than others in the profession. Now Karl Mannheim has argued that the mode of thought and perspective of an individual is 'conditioned by the social situations in which they arose and to which they are relevant'.[59] If this is so, we need to ask how it is that in a class society where one's class position shapes perspectives, some middle-class people like these activists appear to champion the cause of the under class? A partial answer may be found in Mannheim's own discussion of the intelligentsia and their acquisition of a detached perspective through education. Though he refers to them as the 'socially unattached intelligentsia' this is not to imply that they operate within a social vacuum. They retain some affinity with their class of origin and for many intellectuals this is the middle class, but they have a reduced attachment to any one class when compared with those more fully involved in the economy.

It is education which in Mannheim's view transcends the intellectuals' class origins and binds together an otherwise heterogenous group of people: 'Participation in a common educational heritage progressively tends to suppress differences of birth, status, profession and wealth and to unite the individual educated people on the basis of the education they have received.'[60] As noted earlier the experience of education acts in a way similar to inborn characteristics, determining an individual's 'intellectual horizon'; in the case of a social science education enlarging on his appreciation of various social structures and cultural forms and capacity to analyse social conditions.

Mannheim contends that the unattached intellectual has two courses available to take him from the middle of the road position —affiliation with a social class or through recognizing his unique social position embarking on his own mission of political and social change.[61] In the views of Sherwell and Attlee quoted earlier, it would seem that the latter course is the one they are urging for social workers, a concern for principles and not specifically for the well-being of a particular class. With today's social work activists their radical concerns seem more clearly rooted in class conflict. The ability of intellectuals to attach themselves to classes other than those of their origin, arises from their capacity to chose an affiliation and adopt a variety of viewpoints, unlike those who have not escaped from the bonds of class.

Do the activists as described in this essay correspond to the intelligentsia, at least within the social work profession? This question cannot be answered convincingly because of the imprecise nature of the notion of intellectual and the limited data available here. Mannheim's ideas however do provide a useful basis which might be further developed in exploring aspects of yesterday's social reformers and today's social work activists.

In practice, while on the one hand social work attracts women in large numbers because of its oft-presented extension of the female role, on the other its appeal to graduate middle-class radicals could be that it appears as a career more compatible with their focal concerns than those in industry or commerce. Such people, where they express dissatisfaction with present social work practice and recognize the shortcomings of the social services, are the vehicles of reform expression. The continuing recruitment of university social science graduates can contribute to the return of a social movement quality in professional social work. There will be those who will, no doubt, be more influenced by career and domestic concerns, and exercise caution whilst giving service in the name of their employer, lest the latter be offended. Yet their radicalism may spill over into out-of-work activities, being active with client groups and within the professional association.

For the moment, some would urge BASW to be more active as a pressure group for reform. Though there is overlap, a distinction can be drawn between social movement and pressure group based on their approaches to achieving change. This is not to say that pressure groups do not have a movement dimension—it is feasible that reformists or activists within BASW may influence the Association to develop a normative commitment to change and increased participation by members at all levels. BASW is well poised for pressure group activity. Its financial base is secure and it counts amongst its membership, although not a totality of those performing social work tasks, a wealth of talent, knowledge and expertise. However, large size can be a handicap, for the diversity that it brings often leads to bitter internal dissension. A professional association unambiguously committed to, and actively pursuing, social reform seems unlikely, given the plurality of interests and notably the concern of some with adopting 'professional' postures. According to the positions of influence obtained by different interests in the Association, it may lurch from reformism to conservatism in a continuing cycle. The opportunities are greater at branch level for continuing reform activities and one might predict further examples of urban-based branches engaging in campaigns such as the recent Merseyside example of protest over housing policy.[62] Professional social work is becoming gradually aware of its irrelevance for serving the economically and socially disadvantaged, but locked as it is in bureaucratic control and cherishing its traditional focus on the individual, any change will be slow.

Notes

1 P. Seed, *The Expansion of Social Work in Britain*, Routledge & Kegan Paul, 1973, p. 3, This book with its broad historical perspective provides a fuller discussion of the social movement qualities of social work.

2 Professional social work is the expression employed here to distinguish the practice of trained and salaried social workers from others concerned with social work in its broadest sense. Professional is used in relation to those who view themselves as such and can persuade others so to regard them. See D. Feldstein, 'Do we need professions in our society?', *Social Work* (USA), vol. 16, no. 4, October 1971.

3 P. Wilkinson, *Social Movement*, Pall Mall, 1971, p. 11.

4 Ibid., p. 26.

5 Seed, op. cit., chapter 3.

6 A. Sherwell in W. Reason (ed.), *University and Social Settlements*, Methuen, 1898, quoted in Seed, op. cit., p. 36.

7 C. Attlee, *The Social Worker*, Bell, 1920, quoted in A. Sinfield, 'The fifth social service', *Fabian*, 1970, p. 53.

8 R. Lees, *Politics and Social Work*, Routledge & Kegan Paul, 1972, chapter 1.

9 R. Bitensky, 'The influence of political power in determining the theoretical development of social work', *Journal of Social Policy*, vol. 2. no. 2, 1973.

10 Ibid.

11 R. Titmuss, *Commitment to Welfare*, Allen & Unwin, 1968, chapter 13.

12 B. S. Rowntree and G. Lavers, *Poverty and the Welfare State: A Third Social Survey of York Dealing only with Economic Questions*, Longman, 1951.

13 See for example B. Abel-Smith and P. Townsend, *The Poor and the Poorest*, Bell 1965.

14 For example the Government's own surveys, *Finance and other Circumstances of Retirement Pensioners*, Ministry of Pensions and National Insurance, 1966; *Circumstances of Families*, Ministry of Social Security, 1967,

both published by HMSO.

15 See for example B. Plowden (Chairman), *Children and Their Primary Schools*, A Report of the Central Advisory Council for Education, HMSO, 1967.

16 A factor giving rise to the establishment of the Committee on Local Authority and Allied Personal Social Services, F. Seebohm (Chairman), appointed in 1965 'to review the organisational responsibilities of local authority personal social services in England and Wales ...'.

17 R. Perlman and A. Gurin, *Community Organization and Social Planning*, Wiley, 1972, p. 25.

18 J. Richard, 'A radical innocence', *Social Work Today*, vol. 2, no. 9, 1971.

19 F. Seebohm, 'Dole with everything', Radio 4 Broadcast, 23 January 1969, quoted in Sinfield, op. cit., p. 34.

20 See for example, N. Bond, 'The case for radical casework', *Social Work Today*, vol. 2, no. 9, 1971; M. Rein, 'Social work in search of a radical profession', *Social Work* (USA), vol. 15, no. 2, 1970; R. Holman, 'Pressing for social reform', *British Hospital Journal*, 26 July 1968; J. Morrish 'The relevance to agency-based workers of community work and social action', *Social Work Today*, vol. 1, no. 2, 1970.

21 Social Action Working Party Discussion Paper, *Social Work Today*, vol. 2, no. 13, 1971. Social Action here refers to 'various tactics and strategies used to achieve changes in the social situation of individuals, groups and communities'.

22 T. Cooper, Chairman's comment, *Social Work Today*, vol. 3, no. 25, 1973.

23 R. Lees, 'Social action', *New Society*, vol. 18, no. 474, 28 October 1971.

24 As a preliminary to a larger study, a mail questionnaire survey of one of the Welsh branches of BASW was undertaken. A response rate of 50 per cent was obtained and a check on the representativeness of respondents revealed no significant differences between them and the branch membership as a whole. The questionnaire consisted of items relating to the purposes and methods of social work and the role of the professional association. Some of the findings are reported in J. Cypher, 'Sections and strife', *Social Work Today*, vol. 4, no. 4, 1973.

25 J. B. Butterworth (Chairman), *Report of the Butterworth Inquiry into the Work and Pay of Probation Officers and Social Workers*, HMSO, 1972, appendix 11, table 1.

26 C. Meyer, *Social Work Practice: A Response to the Urban Crisis*, Free Press, 1970, p. 53.

27 I. Epstein, 'Professionalization, professionalism and social-worker radicalism', *Journal of Health and Social Behaviour*, vol. 11, no. 1, 1970.

28 Meyer, op. cit., p. 142.

29 See for example B. Varley, 'Socialization and social work education', *Social Work* (USA), vol. 8, no. 3, 1963.

30 R. Bucher and A. Strauss, 'Professions in process', *American Journal of Sociology*, vol. 66, no. 4, 1961.

31 Rein, op. cit.

32 See Cypher, op. cit.

33 BASW was divided into four sections, the purpose of which was to give members some area of familiar meeting in the new association. Each member belongs to at least one section. The sections are:

1 Physical Illness and Handicap
2 Mental Health

3 Child and Family Social Work
4 Treatment of Offenders
The divisiveness arising from the existence of sections is the subject of some debate within BASW. A motion to remove them was defeated at the 1972 Annual General Meeting of BASW.

34 I. Epstein, 'Professionalization and Social Work Activism', unpublished Ph.D. thesis, Graduate Faculty of Political Science, University of Columbia, 1969.

35 Rein, op. cit.

36 J. Parker and R. Allen, 'Social workers in local government', *Social and Economic Administration*, vol. 3, no. 1, January 1969.

37 A. Billingsley, 'Bureaucratic and professional orientation patterns in social casework', *Social Service Review*, vol. 38, no. 4, 1964.

38 D. McLeod and H. Meyer, 'A Study of the Values of Social Workers', in E. Thomas (ed.), *Behavioral Science for Social Workers*, Free Press, 1967.

39 J. Rea Price, 'Hierarchy and management style: 1', *British Hospital Journal*, 6 November 1971.

40 W. Scott, 'Professional Employees in a Bureaucratic Structure: Social Work, in A. Etzioni (ed.), *The Semi-Professions and their Organization*, Free Press, 1969.

41 See Billingsley, op. cit.

42 F. Sytz, 'The Folklore of Social Work', quoted in Scott, op. cit.

43 F. Ruderman, 'Sex Differences: Biological, Cultural, Societal Implications', in C. Epstein and W. Goode (eds), *The Other Half*, Prentice-Hall, 1971.

44 J. Bardwick, *Psychology of Women*, Harper & Row, 1971, p. 162.

45 Ibid.

46 See B. Barber, *Social Stratification*, Harcourt Brace & Co., 1957, especially chapters 14 and 15.

47 R. Simpson and I. Simpson, 'Women and Bureaucracy in the Semi-Professions', in Etzioni (ed.), op. cit.

48 R. Merton, *Social Theory and Social Structure*, Free Press, 1957, p. 265

49 Ibid., p. 266.

50 B. Jackson and D. Marsden, *Education and the Working Class*, Routledge & Kegan Paul, 1962.

51 M. Riley and A. Foner, *Aging and Society, Vol. 1: An Inventory of Research Findings*, Russell Sage, 1968, chaps 12 and 19.

52 Lees, op. cit.

53 V. Schein, 'Personality Dimensions and Need', in Riley and Foner, op. cit., chap. 12.

54 Riley and Foner, op. cit.

55 See Simpson and Simpson, op. cit.

56 See F. Parkin, *Middle Class Radicalism*, Manchester University Press, 1968, p. 170.

57 Ibid., p. 171.

58 J. Adelson, quoted in A. Robins, 'Constraints on innovation in social work education', *Applied Social Studies*, vol. 3, no. 3, 1971.

59 K. Mannheim, *Ideology and Utopia*, Kegan Paul, Trench, Trubner, 1936, p. 255.

60 Ibid., pp. 136-46.

61 Ibid., p. 138.

62 'Merseyside on housing', *Social Work Today*, vol. 4, no. 3, 1973, p. 82.

3

Social workers and political action
Geoffrey Mungham

Introduction

To what type of social formation do social workers belong? Most writers would probably place them in the ranks of the 'professions' or, perhaps—following Etzioni[1]—the 'semi-professions'. From this view the relationship between social work and political action becomes a search for those political modes and styles compatible with 'professionalism'.

For my part, I shall argue that the 'social character' of social work requires a more inclusive definition than this, if we are to comprehend its politics. Social work, it is true, has the aspect of a profession but it also, I believe, possesses some of the salient features of both a bureaucracy and a social movement. In short, social work is a kind of prism, the refracting surfaces of which (profession, bureaucracy, social movement) comprise the framework for any discussion of political action and social work.

A common tendency among those who have tried to determine the nature of the relationship between social workers and political action has been to substitute in place of analysis some programmatic statements about the kind of political tactics thought appropriate for 'radical' social workers.[2] Such presentations rest upon the assumption, confidently made, that we know all we need to know about the essential character of the social work profession. This easy confidence might be defensible with regard to the profession in the USA (where every social worker would seem to have appeared in at least one PhD student's sample survey population), but there are few who would be willing to make a similar claim about the profession of social work in this country.

With this in mind then, the aims of this paper are simply stated. To establish the major social characteristics of the social work profession in England and Wales; to examine those factors which are, at present, forcing an expansion and redefinition of social work; and to see to what extent these patterns of structural change can be associated with the emergence of different forms of occupational attitudes and behaviour (including 'radical' orientations) among those social workers affected by the new arrangements. In other words, to try to find out just what kind of social formation it *is* that we are all so ready to pronounce judgment on and then, and only then, start talking of its relationship with 'politics'.

Social work as a bureaucracy and a profession

Social workers are members of a segmental profession. This term, borrowed from an essay by Bucher and Strauss on the internal stratification of the American medical profession, refers to the way in which:[3]

> In actuality, the assumption of relative homogeneity within [a] profession is not entirely useful: there are many identities, many values and many interests. These amount not merely to differentiation or simple variation. They tend to become patterned and shared; coalitions develop and flourish—and in opposition to some others. ... We shall develop the idea of professions as loose amalgamations of segments pursuing different objectives in different manners and more or less delicately held together under a common name at a particular period in history.

If we concede, as I think we must, that this formula fits social work very well, then we have also to concede that the use of the term, the 'social work profession' (with its suggestion of unity and homogeneity) only serves to misrepresent reality. This point is introduced since no discussion of the styles of political action appropriate for social work—or, more accurately, for segments of its membership—can be seriously entered into until these basic social facts are understood. Accordingly, I want first to review briefly the changing market and work situation of social workers. Among the principal features are: (1) changing patterns of recruitment; this means not only a rising graduate entry, but also an increase in the number of graduate entrants with specific professional social work qualifications; (2) a sharp increase in the total number of social workers, with a resultant shift in the age-profile of the social work profession; (3) a changed market situation; thus with the reorganisation of local authority social services following the guidelines laid down by Seebohm,[4] the career structure for qualified social workers has been radically changed;[5] (4) a changed work situation; the Seebohm proposals, combined with the increase in the numbers of social workers, has resulted in a growing concentration of social workers in group and area work teams;[6] (5) changes in the system and content of the training programme; the observations I shall want to make here are necessarily rather speculative (in the absence of any reliable empirical accounts), yet there are some signs that professional training for social work places less emphasis now on a Freudian ideology and its variants, and more on the political problems raised by the organisational changes which have been hinted at, and by the current vague vogue notions of 'community work'; (6) the emergence of new forms of career and occupational consciousness among social workers and which partially reflect the situations outlined above;[7] (7) the effect of bringing together in the new social service departments people with very different amounts of training and very different kinds of previous work experiences—creating unsolved status problems and problems of unification.

It was thought by Seebohm that the career structure 'might broadly evolve as follows',[8] beginning with a basic grade for all professionally qualified social workers. The next step was to be a senior social worker position in area teams, before finally moving on to a wide range of senior—mainly administrative—posts. There was a call too for the simplification and rationalisation of training procedures, and for the abolition of the differences (in career chances and professional status) between those university trained social workers on the one hand, and those trained elsewhere on the other.

It was a measure of the success of Seebohm that most of the proposals relating to reorganisation and career structures were quickly taken up, if not always swiftly implemented. But the creation of a unitary career structure has not—as yet—been accompanied by a resolution of the problem of a fragmented system of training. Indeed the rapid organisational changes involved have posed problems of adjustment for training courses, increasing uncertainty about aims and methods. There is, thus far, no agreement on the correct place for, and content of, a 'proper' professional education for social work. As a consequence, the new monolithic social service departments continue to be serviced by several different types of training institutions that between them award a range of degrees, diplomas and certificates of varying quality and status.[9] The significance of this kind of 'occupational lag' for social work professionals lies in its implications for the stratification of these work groups. There has been, first of all, strong disagreement and resentment within the profession over the criteria sometimes used for selection to the highest positions in the newly-integrated social services. And second, the stratification of the system of professional education has been a major factor in granting differential access to the variety of career lines which are open to

SOCIAL WORKERS AND POLITICAL ACTION

social workers today. Let us now consider these issues in detail.

The Seebohm Committee were anxious to remove all distinctions between professionally qualified university entrants and those entrants trained elsewhere, in social work. However, in practice, reorganisation has not only preserved the traditional hierarchy among professionally qualified social workers (i.e. the pre-eminence of university personnel), but in addition a number of the new senior posts are being awarded to graduates lacking even social work qualifications. There is emerging in fact in some areas something akin to an 'administrative' or 'executive' class in the new departments, whose training in and direct experience of social work is often hard to discern.[10]

Finally we should give brief mention to the factors of rising graduate recruitment, and the overall increase in the number of full-time welfare professionals. Not only is the graduate entry to social work increasing—but it would also seem that the rise is linked to parallel negative career choice processes elsewhere. That is, the generally poor job-market for graduates is having the effect, not surprisingly, of boosting recruitment to the welfare professions with their promise of securer employment than can be found in the private sector.

An important feature of the general increase in numbers is the rising numbers of men entrants to social work. They are attracted, we may suppose, by the improved market situation, and salaries and status of work in this sector—together of course with the pressure on graduate employment elsewhere. But whatever the reason, I would suggest that changes in the sex-composition of the work force may be a powerful factor in encouraging the emergence of new forms of career and occupational consciousness among these professionals.

There can be little doubt that the emergence of the new social services departments has created, objectively, quite different market and work (and, obliquely, status) situations for welfare professionals. The central problem now remaining is to interpret the sources of their subjective perceptions of these changes as a way of understanding the development of militancy among them.

Paradoxically, reorganisation has played an important part in the current militant attitudes and behaviour of some welfare professionals who were not directly affected by the Seebohm proposals. A good case in point is provided by probation officers. They were not included in the Seebohm terms of reference; consequently the new social services departments have been developed without any reference to them. In this way, therefore, the improved salaries and career structures for qualified staff which the new service offers are formally denied to probation officers.[11] As a result of these emerging differentials, the probation service is currently going through a phase of militancy—predicated on the demands for higher pay and better conditions of service.[12] The dispute is an interesting one because it also involves a strong measure of inter-professional rivalry; in this case between the newly formed British Association of Social Workers (BASW) and the National Association of Probation Officers (NAPO).

At this stage it is useful to distinguish between what may be termed 'inner' and 'outer' directed militancy among social workers. Militancy of the former type may be defined as a concern over salaries and conditions of work—in other words with a narrow range of occupational objectives. The latter type, by contrast, refers to the concern with client and 'social policy' affairs. The two types are by no means mutually exclusive. A simple example will suffice here. Thus a campaign to improve salaries may be justified on the familiar grounds that more and better recruits will be attracted thereby, to the ultimate benefit of the client and the community. Arguments of this kind have, as is well known, been liberally employed by schoolteachers in this country in recent drives to raise their salaries.

Although we have yet to see a large-scale 'mobilisation' of social workers for 'inner' and 'outer' directed militancy, one observable —and unintended—consequence of reorganisation will be to make this sort of action easier than hitherto. Thus the concentration of social workers in larger work units together with the present emphasis on work in teams makes communication easier between those so affected, and *what* they are able to communicate better are those common experiences and sentiments which derive from a shared work situation. At the same time, the improved salary and career structures are factors in encouraging more men than before to enter social work (indeed, to enter the welfare professions in general). And, as is well known,[13] a shift in the social demography of an occupation can have a profound effect upon the degree and content of its militancy.

There are two factors, above all, that I would like to draw attention to here: the system of training for the welfare professions, and the influence of wider political forces and decisions upon the situation of these groups.

First then, the training system, where the incumbent's occupational identity and self-image are mediated through both the formal and informal mechanisms of this aspect of the professional socialisation process. The obverse side of this coinage is the impact of the internal occupational changes that I have just described, upon the nature of professional education, considered in its broadest sense. These involve both 'formal' education (in the sense of changing course content) and 'informal' education (socialisation into the student—'pre-professional'—culture, which helps shape students' perceptions of the occupational world they are destined for), and which are enacted at each level simultaneously.

New forms of course content are a significant development because they not only acknowledge changes in the basic orientations and modes of work of social workers, but in recognising them, *legitimise* them. The direction of instruction and pedagogy is slowly away from more traditional personal, therapeutic concerns, towards rather more impersonal, social-structural orientations. As the Freudian ideology and its variants lose ground in professional training, so social workers turn increasingly to notions (vague as yet) of 'community work' and programmes for collective action. And there is a growing tendency now for social work trainees to have their placements not in the usual casework agencies, but among the rapidly proliferating 'community action' schemes.

The revision of training programmes may then be seen as one way of coping both with the contingencies of social service reorganisation, as well as enabling present social workers to compete against, or work more productively with, those radical reform groups working on the margins of the 'welfare industry'.

There is a final point to consider on professional education. Some of the present militancy among young social workers has been explained in terms of a reaction to, or a dissatisfaction with, the organisation and content of the system of training. I doubt if such a relationship exists; or if it does, then I would argue that it would only hold under certain special conditions. The work of Kuhn[14] suggests what these circumstances might be. According to Kuhn, even extremely high levels of dissatisfaction with the quality of professional education on the part of those receiving it, will seldom provoke serious protest provided the newly qualified practitioner has access to secure professional employment and a high level of financial reward (or the hope of such). It is these factors, for example, which have successfully 'cooled out' generations of law and medical students, among whom discontent over courses has traditionally been high.

Dissatisfaction about course content among social work students is most commonly manifested in terms of a demand for 'relevant' course material, i.e. 'relevant' to the immediate day-to-day concerns of doing social work. Such demands are often most strongly articulated by radical students in these fraternities. The fact that these requests are usually met does not herald the radicalisation of social work training, but its increasing *professionalisation*. This point may only be understood if student pressures for course reform are linked with those issues that are currently dividing the staff who teach in schools and departments of social work. Briefly, the tension here is between those, on the one hand, who prefer a good measure of 'generic' social science teaching to social work students; and on the other hand, those—usually staff holding professional social work qualifications—who are pressing for an increasing, if not total, 'professionalisation' of social work training, i.e. courses that relate directly and practically to the 'technical skills' of social work. And it is this last group that provide a sympathetic hearing for the opinion of radical students. Viewed from this perspective, therefore, the pressure from students, which often has its genesis in some kind of radical critique of the social work profession, for 'relevant' courses, has the paradoxical result of strengthening the hand of those who want to force the development of a highly professionalised social work—whose orientation and residual loyalties may well prove to be anything but 'radical'. In this way, then, the militant sentiments of students are co-opted and comfortably accommodated within pre-existing professional, organisational and ideological structures.

Next, social work and the general political process. The social services are clearly an area where party political struggles—local and national—are forceful and often vindictive. As Cohen has pointed out, reorganisation has meant a new set of bureaucratic constraints on the professional activities of social workers and their attempts to link up with outside groups are usually resisted by employers and by local politicians. Thus:[15]

> A number of recent developments have led part of the new
> generation of social workers in this country to become
> very aware of tensions and contradictions previously latent in
> their situation. As the rhetoric of social policy leans
> towards greater integration of the social services, so the
> political problems raised by such organisational changes
> become more apparent; as often as the consensus about the
> welfare state is repeated, so ways of coping with 'new'
> problems such as child poverty become subject to deep
> disagreements ... as social workers struggle to operate
> within statutory frameworks, such as those of local authorities,
> so the successes of groups working outside these frameworks
> (such as squatters dealing with housing problems)
> become more manifest.

But if these are examples of the ways in which new developments and orientations have affected the professional consciousness of social workers, there still remains the even more interesting case of changes in occupational consciousness being effected by the *absence* of political 'interference'. I refer here to the process through which many social workers are attempting to mobilise the poor and the exploited, because the Labour Party and the trade unions no longer appear capable of doing such work. This point was made rather polemically by Rose,[16] but documented in rigorous detail in a recent book on working-class politics.[17]

Action of this type is a characteristic of twilight inner-city zones, where redevelopment has left behind a rump of what were once large, working-class communities. These residual populations, alienated from the main political parties (especially Labour), have evolved extra-party political strategies for action. And these projects, focusing as they usually do on tenancy and welfare issues, attract social workers as aides.

Finally, I would argue that the increasing evidence that social workers are taking initiatives in this way, confirms their growing strength, visibility and confidence. These actions cannot be explained solely in terms of the contradictions thrown up by traditional professional ideologies in social work. For many years now some social workers have been aware of the need to define their place in a pluralistic society—either (to over-simplify the matter) as agents in the control of deviancy or as advocates of the underprivileged. The significance of current developments lies in the fact that the structure of the profession is, itself, changing, and along the lines I earlier described. And it is this conjunction of events which makes it possible effectively to sustain these 'new' forms of action.

Militancy and social work professionalism*

Changes in the organisation of Social Services departments following Seebohm, the formation of BASW and national and regional Case-Con groups, the alignment of some social workers with social activists such as squatters associations, the Claimants Union, and community law centres, the advent of organised community work, could all be interpreted as indices of the internal contradictions of social work theory and practice. The contradictions are the subject of vigorous discussion both by practitioners and educators within social work concerning the fundamental question of what social workers are and what they ought to be doing. Underlying this discussion are different modes of explanation of social behaviour (psychology, psychoanalytic theories of development, and so on) and structural explanations of social behaviour (mainly derived from structural–functionalist and marxist brands of sociological theory). These individual and structural theories tend to be seen

* I am indebted to Roger Evans for many of the ideas presented in this section of my paper.

as mutually exclusive competitors when seeking explanations of clients' problems: [18]

> Social Science cannot offer a sufficient understanding of the individual person in relation to his life situations. As a result we are impelled to make a choice between personality and social structure, although it is obvious that what we require is not a choice but an integrated theory.

An important consequence of this distinction is a parallel distinction between modes of social intervention. The individual explanations are related to a casework method which is seen by its critics as ignoring the social–structural dimensions of clients' problems. Caseworkers, and thereby social workers, are seen as the agents of social control for advantaged groups within a social structure which is differentiated with respect to various forms of inequality (power, wealth, etc.) and within which the client is inevitably located in the disadvantaged group. Alternatively, structural explanations are related to modes of intervention that are aimed primarily at providing a change in the client's situation of which the most obvious example is community work. However, one could claim that this is to impose a false dichotomy on both the theoretical and practical alternatives available. For example, the recent concern among sociologists with interactionalist social psychology and phenomenological sociology is an attempt to take account of individual behaviour within the context of social structure.[19] Similarly attempts to devise a radical casework technique[20] indicate that modes of intervention are not mutually exclusive. What is apparent is that the issues are more complex than the structural–individual dichotomy would suggest.

It is interesting then to note the increasing reference both in newspaper reports on the activities of social workers and in the social work journals to the division of the occupation into two clear-cut groups labelled 'professionals' and 'radicals'. These groups are often referred to as if their membership was readily identifiable and as if they were necessarily opposed in their aims for social work. In their most extreme form these stereotypes are represented as follows. The professional stereotype is seen as having a central concern with the development of casework theory and practice that will enable him to stake a legitimate claim to the possession of a skill unique to the occupation and suitable as a basis for professionalisation. Evidence for this professional aspiration is seen in the formation of a professional association (BASW) and its attempts to obtain those characteristics that the established professions are thought to have (a code of ethics, a unique body of knowledge, control over entry to the occupation and training, and so on). Alternatively, the radical stereotype is seen as opposed to casework, possibly committed to community work and certainly committed to a programme of socio-political action within the occupation, aimed at a broad attack on the inegalitarian nature of society that is considered to be at the root of social problems. This programme is to be pursued in alignment with the trade-union movement (in particular NALGO) and socialist revolutionary groups.

The emergence of these stereotypes raises a number of interesting questions, particularly with regard to their origins. One could regard them as emerging through the process of typification.[21] In other words, the way in which practising social workers who may experience the contradictions inherent in their occupational activities give order to the apparent disorder of their experience by giving a rational account of it. These contradictions may occur at a number of points in the social worker's interaction both with clients and with colleagues. For example they might become apparent in experiencing the limited value of psychotherapeutic casework with clients who are in situations of extreme material deprivation; in the social transactions which the caseworker may have with community workers who share responsibility for clients in the same area; or in the conflicting demands of social work courses, designed to educate students for a role in the social services and at the same time equip them to produce changes in that role when appropriate. Given these contradictions the rationalisation process occurs in the construction of alternative accounts of occupational behaviour which are encapsulated in the radical and professional stereotypes. These typifications can be seen as folk sociological categories creating social order through giving logically consistent, i.e. rational, accounts of inherently contradictory and confused social inter-actions. Of course this begs the question of what exact processes underlie the creation of these typifications and why these should have emerged rather than possible alternatives.

The important point is that having once been created, these categories then become reified and as a consequence radicals and professionals within the occupation are seen as alternative realities rather than alternative explanations of the same reality. In this way some social workers appear to act as if they were in some way obliged to choose between membership of what they identify as the radical and professional group and between radical and professional modes of intervention.

If this type of explanation has any merit, then a number of research problems suggest themselves. First, there is the question of whether these categories are considered as social realities by practising social workers (as opposed to social work educators or writers). Similarly, it would be useful to establish whether the

35

meanings attached to these categories varied systematically among members of different groups within social work. One could, for instance, ask with Epstein whether the meanings varied systematically according to occupational specialism and organisational position. Second, one could ask whether radicals and professionals were simply identified in the minds of social workers through their membership of what may be considered radical or professional organisations. For instance, radical social workers may simply be equated with supporters of the Case-Con organisation. Alternatively these categories may be seen not as structural components but as differing attitudes towards the role. Third, it would be necessary to explain why professionalism is contrasted with radicalism with its implication that professional aspirations and values are inherently conservatising.

This stark dichotomy has, I would argue, little analytical value and, further, has won no serious empirical support. What should properly be the focus of interest here is not the attempt to isolate 'polar-types' of work orientation (which anyway is the basis only for a *non-dynamic* model for the study of this form of militancy), but instead to establish the degree of legitimacy given to the use of militant techniques by different groups acting within the same profession at any one time. There is no obvious reason at all why militant action should be regarded as incompatible with the pursuit of orthodox professional goals, though in cases of this kind, the task of conceptualisation is enormously complicated by the problem of the contrasting *meanings* which those involved employ in order to rationalise their notions. Hence for many professionals the struggle to establish a proper code of practice may not be seen as 'militant' action at all. Indeed, in cases such as these, occupational incumbents often go to great lengths to avoid the usual language of conflict situations.

For researchers, then, it becomes not only a question of being able to construct some way of assessing differing degrees of militant behaviour; they have also to grapple with the respondents' subjective perception of that action that we may categorise as 'militant'. The fact that some social workers are now apparently willing to forswear the paraphernalia of professionalism, whilst retaining a keen interest in improving the clients' quality of life is, I think, of importance. It suggests, first of all, that their reference groups are changing—which may have far-reaching consequences for their future occupational attitudes and behaviour. And second, I would argue that, in the absence or rejection in such cases of any constraining professional ethic, we shall continue to see the emergence of new forms of 'outer-directed' militant action designed to serve the clients' interests.[22] Such action need not be interpreted as 'political'; or at least, it is doubtful if all those actually involved would see it as such. One consequence of these developments would almost certainly be a further weakening of the internal cohesiveness of the welfare professions. These groups, always vulnerable to ideological appeals,[23] are put under considerable pressure by the pattern of current events.

Social work as a social movement

How might this label be justified for social work? Banks has argued that a not uncommon characteristic of specific organisations is a vague '... *conscience collective* that gives support to such bodies in the communities where they are found'.[24]

Gusfield has made the point well:[25]

> There is a mixture of formal association and informal, diffuse behaviour encompassed in the concept of a movement. A significant distinction can be made between 'directed' and 'undirected' movements or segments of movements. The *directed* segment of a movement is characterised by organised and structural groups with specific programs, a formal leadership structure, definitive ideology, and stated objectives. Its followers are *members* of an organisation as well as partisans to a belief. The *undirected* phase of a movement is characterised by the reshaping of perspectives, norms and values which occur in the interaction of persons apart from a specific vocational context. The followers are *partisan* but need not be members of any association which advocates the change being studied.

Social work has been and is represented by the different phases and segments that Gusfield describes. The concern of some sections of the 'movement' has always been as much with the moral improvement of society, as it has with supplying a specific ameliorative service. This abiding interest in what one author has called 'the moral reformation of society[26] gives social work the flavour of a social movement. If we grant this then social work is very much a movement of a ' "cause" pressure group' kind.[27] That is, social movement in the sense:[28]

> that their members, and especially their leaders, usually have a fairly clear idea of the form viable organisations must take for the purpose of social change; and to the degree that they succeed in persuading the government to move, their conceptions become the chief organisational elements in the administrative system which is eventually created.

Banks goes on to point out that the existence of social movements of this type depends upon three factors:[29]

> (1) the readiness of the population and its masters to tolerate social experimentation by some members of a society; (2) the willingness of governments to undertake positive experiment-ation of this kind themselves; and (3) the possibility that governments will allow themselves to be persuaded by some members of society to experiment in ways which the govern-ments themselves had not thought of. The era of 'cause' pressure-group movements, that is to say, is the era of the welfare state, or more accurately the era of the social service state which preceded it.

As a social movement and a rapidly growing social formation, social work cannot claim for itself any unambiguous relationship to 'political action'. At the global level (i.e. putting aside, for the moment, the issue of how the individual social worker formulates his own politics), for example, will—as Gartner and Reissman put it—'the new service society vanguards move towards a human-istic socialism or some new forms of egalitarianism or will they become a new élite?'[30] To take this further, it is not hard to envisage social work fighting on more than one political front. First, as a participant in the struggle over the allocation of state and local government resources and to maintain autonomy from those who fund it. And second, to preserve and expand its own con-stituency. Social workers are peculiarly vulnerable to 'consumer control' or what Johnson calls 'communal patronage';[31] a devolution that receives some encouragement from elements in the profes-sional ideology of social work itself. Indeed, for some segments inside social work the only effective social work practice is that which will serve to destroy the very basis of social work as a profession.

Conclusion

The social work profession is going through a period of expansion and redefinition. The changing social characteristics of social workers, together with the reorganisation of the work and market (career) situation of social work (which I described in the first part of the paper), seem to suggest that the scale of militancy in the profession will increase rather than decrease, at least so long as the growth of social work is maintained. This rider is introduced because one of the precipitating factors in professional militancy would seem to be the buoyancy of the job market. This suggests a kind of 'market-model' as an explanation of the genesis of their militancy; without making exaggerated claims for this interpretation, the evidence (and it applies to professions other than that of social work)[32] would seem to indicate that a highly favourable —for incumbents—market situation encourages a more general support for 'outer-directed' militancy, as well as more obviously making it easier to organise for militancy of the 'inner-directed' kind. In fact, in a market situation of this kind, when recruits are difficult to get, there is often little need for militancy of the latter type, since employers will themselves tend to take the initiative in raising salaries, etc., to make the work more attractive.

However, this factor alone cannot determine the outcome and character of social worker militancy. Some role, for instance, would have to be given in the development of militancy among social workers to their experience of the poor conditions in which many of their clients live. I have already mentioned the effect of social work being a 'segmental' profession. Next there is no sign yet that social workers (or rather, groups within the occupation who are oriented towards 'outer-directed' militancy) have been able to find allies or any kind of 'natural constituency' for political or social reform work,[33] even though individual social workers can and do choose to support recognised welfare pressure groups such as the Child Poverty Action Group and Shelter (all this is not to deny that BASW has been active as a reformist pressure group from its inception). As a social movement, segmental profession, and bureaucracy, social work is both the subject and promulgator of cross-cutting political actions and tensions. Several different dimensions of this conflict have been suggested in this paper and may be summarised in the following way:

A 'Internal Politics'
1 segmental conflicts

2 bureaucratic v. professional interests

B 'External Politics'
1 social work v. the state and local authorities
2 social work v. other professions (the territorial imperative)
3 social work v. the consumer

The process of social work mirrors these discrepant tendencies which underlines the complexity of its political involvements. While some of these conflicts may be affected by other issues (for example, segmental conflicts may be hidden beneath a shared interest among all social workers in resisting encroachment from, say, local authorities), there is no prospect, as yet, of a general and lasting peace. In part, the confused relationship between social work and political action reflects the 'fragmentary' character of social work; but it also reflects the uncertainties of contemporary British politics. Historically the welfare professions (with teachers as the example par excellence) have generally sought as their *patron* the Labour party, recognising some convergence of interests between themselves and Labour. While this bond will still be preferred by many social workers there are, today, no compelling reasons why they should expect the modern Labour movement to be the faithful carriers of social work ideologies and interests.

In the long run the 'political' social worker will have—unless he elects to abandon the profession altogether—to bring a flavour of politics into the ordinary everyday practice of his social work. And this can be done not by ignoring established professional ideologies, or the orthodox canons of 'professionalism', but by drawing upon them selectively, in order to legitimise their own behaviour as radicals. A detailed consideration of these matters is not possible here, but in its most general prospect, a distinctive quality which must be accounted for in the notions of radicalism emerging out of the 1960s is a concern with *radical professionalism*, as opposed to professionals who lead 'radical' private lives. If my understanding of the issue is correct, it is the merging of life-style and political conviction in the politics of the New Left which provides a model of what it is to be a radical social worker, going beyond a comprehension of him as a social worker who also happens to hold certain beliefs. It is 'five-to-nine radicalism'—of the social worker who sells 'left' newspapers at the factory gate, but plays the autocrat in relationships with clients—which makes it necessary to provide a conceptualisation of 'radical social work' as such. Which is not to say that the quest for radical professionalism, in the sense which I understand it, is necessarily a valid one. There are those who consider the juxtaposition of 'radical' and 'professional' bizarre, and it takes little imagination to see their case. It is, however, my contention that insufficient groundwork has been done on the relationship to make such easy pronouncements possible. Whatever the practicalities of the phenomenon, the aspiration is real enough, and we find that in its general form others concur with the argument set out here:[34]

> Part-time radicalism was one of the crucial elements in the
> failure of the old-left. A commitment to radical politics must
> mean a commitment to a style of life which is congruent.
> Ideology which is not tested and practised in everyday behaviour
> will inescapably become unworkable and brittle with age.
> Integral to the radicalism of the new left is the struggle for a
> new life.

Notes

1 A. Etzioni, *The Semi-Professions and Their Organization: Teachers,*

Nurses and Social Workers, Free Press, New York, 1969.

2 Two recent examples will suffice. Rein has identified four 'major professional creeds' for social work, viz. (1) traditional casework (2) radical casework (3) community sociotherapy and (4) radical social policy—his own preference being a 'radical casework approach' (M. Rein, 'Social work in search of a radical profession, *Social Work*, vol. 15, 1970, pp. 13-28). More recently still Specht has defined four dominant intellectual currents running through contemporary social work—activism, anti-individualism, communalism and environmental determinism. The origins of each of these strands are not discussed, nor the type of social worker likely to set out along these different paths. (See 'The Deprofessionalisation of Social Work' in *Social Work*, March 1972.)

3 R. Bucher and A. Strauss, 'Professions in process', *American Journal of Sociology*, vol. 66, 1960-1, pp. 325-34.

4 The relevant sources here are as follows: *Annual Reports*, Central Training for Social Work; *Report of the Butterworth Inquiry into the Work and Pay of Probation Officers and Social Workers*, Cmnd 5076 HMSO, 1972; *Report of the Committee On Local Authority and Allied Personal Social Services*, Cmnd 3703, HMSO, 1960; A. Sinfield, 'Which way for social work?', *Fabian Tract 393*, 1969; E. Younghusband, 'Social work manpower and social services', *British Hospital Journal and Social Science Review*, 7 August, 1971; N. Timms, *Social Work*, Routledge & Kegan Paul, 1970.

5 These developments, pleasing as they are to social workers, by no means exhaust the opportunities now open to them. Thus with the current interest in social work 'counselling' there exist more openings than probably ever before for lecturing/teaching work in institutions such as universities, polytechnics, colleges of education, secondary schools, etc.

6 See note 4.

7 The concepts of what I have chosen to call 'career consciousness' and 'occupational consciousness' need clarification, since they appear elsewhere in this paper. Career consciousness refers to the individual's perception of his career chances. Occupational consciousness, however, encompasses more than attitudes towards careers. If occupational consciousness is defined as the sum of the individual worker's perceptions of his total work situation, then we can regard career consciousness as but one aspect of it. In this way we are able to explain the 'contradictions' which are frequently encountered among certain social workers between the objective features of their work situation, and their subjective perceptions of their situation (e.g. those cases where low salary and poor career chances are associated with a high level of commitment to a 'professional' ideology which places a low priority on any collective action to improve the professional's situation). The processes that shape occupational consciousness, like those determining career consciousness, are complex. Their origins are only partly to be explained in terms of events inside particular professions or occupations. It is reasonable to seek for some of the sources in the factors of the individual's family and community background. So far, I have only suggested ways in which occupational consciousness may serve to 'constrain' career consciousness, e.g. those situations where the individual faced with, say, deteriorating career prospects, may give expression to a militant form of career consciousness, but is constrained by his occupational consciousness from 'acting it out'; as well as those examples where occupational consciousness completely denies the emergence of that kind of career consciousness which might be expected to evolve from the concrete circumstances of work. Taking this further, it is certainly not difficult to imagine a conjunction

of events (such as serious personal career setbacks) where a radically transformed career situation is responsible for a general 'crisis of consciousness'
for the individual, leading not only to new forms of career consciousness,
but generating a new occupational consciousness as well.

8 Seebohm, op. cit., p. 162.

9 For example, among them we can count as recognised professional
qualifications, degrees, diplomas or certificates in applied social studies, and
professional qualifications for child care, family casework, medical and
psychiatric social work, the probation and aftercare service and a few
certificates of the Council for training in social work (source: *BASW News*,
1 January 1971). Others able to engage in social work include graduates
and holders of Declarations of Recognition of Experience, as well as those
with qualifications in teaching, nursing or any profession ancillary to
medicine.

10 This is a sensitive issue and has recently attracted a good deal of
publicity. Thus the appointments of non-social workers to directorships of
the new departments in places like Enfield, Ealing, Lindsey and Merthyr
caused much resentment among 'rank-and-file' social workers. At the same
time the most highly qualified tend not to see overmuch of the clients. As
Sinfield has put it: 'The general impression is that the higher the training,
the higher up the career structure the worker starts and the faster he
climbs it. The less trained therefore are most likely to make the first and
continuing contact with clients' (op. cit. p 21). Against this view it can be
argued that there are now more trained social workers at field level than
ever before, because of the expansion of training.

11 The point about careers is particularly important. The probation service
has always offered only a poor career structure for recruits. There were few
promotions available to senior positions, and no clearly delineated career
line as such. There are more senior posts now.

12 'I sense now, in the probation service, an unprecedented bitterness
and desperation—a mood of militancy which is quite extraordinary. ...
Unless something is done quickly I fear ... massive defections to other
social work departments' (from a speech by the chairman of NAPO, reported
in the *Guardian*, 3 March 1971). Allowing for the hyperbole, there is still
little doubt that militant sentiments are, at present, running strongly through
the probation service. The quotation I have used here also indicates the
source of many of the current dissatisfactions, viz. the reorganised social
services departments.

13 See Etzioni, op. cit.; S. Cole, *The Unionisation of Teachers*, Praeger,
1969.

14 T. S. Kuhn, *The Structure of Scientific Revolutions*, University of
Chicago Press, 1971.

15 S. Cohen (ed.), *Images of Deviance*, Penguin, 1971, p. 249. There are
several articles on this theme. Issues of this kind are not simply confined to
'fringe' radical social work journals such as *Case-Con*; they are also
regularly written about in the mainstream professionals, such as *Social
Work Today* and the *British Journal of Social Work*. The social work
profession is characterised by a great deal of confusion over ideology,
skills and appropriate modes of practice. This was demonstrated in the
recent struggles over welfare issues at Islington and Hackney.

16 Rose, op. cit.

17 B. Hindess, *The Decline of Working Class Politics*, MacGibbon & Kee,
1970.

18 M. Rein, op. cit.

19 See, for example, R. Filmer *et al.*, *New Directions in Sociological Theory*, Collier-Macmillan, 1970; and P. Berger and T. Luckmann, *The Social Construction of Reality*, Penguin, 1971.

20 For example, Rein, op. cit., and N. Bond, 'The case for radical casework', *Social Work Today*, vol. 2, no. 9, 1971.

21 For a discussion of the concept of typification, see A. Schütz, *Collected Papers II: Studies in Social Theory*, ed. A. Broderson, Nijhoff, The Hague, 1964, pp. 29-30.

22 One such strategy, which has been expounded in *Case-Con* is that of 'client refusal'. In the words of one of its principal advocates: 'social workers should *refuse to accept the client*. That is, the social worker should refuse to accept the client as client, in whom he proceeds to look for symptoms, or on whom he proceeds to write a case report. Rather, the social worker should accept the new "cases" continually being thrown up by the crises of the system as political allies' (see I. Taylor, 'Client refusal: a political strategy for social work', *Case-Con*, no. 7, April 1972).

23 Thus members of the helping professions are peculiarly prone to appeals 'to help humanity', and no group is probably more self-critical and doubting of the methods it uses. In these circumstances, it is never usually very difficult to find some support for new modes of action.

24 J. A. Banks, *The Sociology of Social Movements*, Macmillan, 1973, p. 13.

25 J. R. Gusfield, 'Social Movements II: The Study of Social Movements', in D. L. Sills (ed.), *International Encyclopedia of the Social Sciences*, Macmillan, 1968, vol. xiv, p. 445.

26 P. Halmos, *The Personal Service Society*, Constable, 1970, esp. ch. 3.

27 Banks, op. cit., p. 26.

28 Ibid., p. 26.

29 Banks, op. cit., p. 26.

30 D. Gartner and F. Reissman, 'Notes on the service society', *Social Policy*, May/June 1973, p. 67.

31 T. Johnson, *Professions and Power*, Macmillan, 1972.

32 For example, I have attempted elsewhere to link the emergence of a 'radicalised sociology' in Britain and the USA to the situation prevailing in the academic market place in the 1960s, while pointing out that an understanding of the specific form of radicalism must be sought elsewhere (this holds, of course, for social work as well). See, G. Mungham and G. Pearson, 'Radical Action and Radical Scholarship', mimeographed paper read at the National Deviancy Conference, University of York, January 1972. It is not difficult to predict that this interpretation will not be a popular one. There must be few people in social work who are prepared publicly to associate variations in their commitment to radicalism with shifts in their market situation; for obvious enough reasons, other kinds of rationalisations are preferred. In this respect, then, the characteristic features of social worker radicalism introduced here are nearly all associated with the profession in an *age of expansion*. Under other conceivable conditions (e.g. reduction in welfare funds, reduced recruitment) the objectives of radical social workers may become rather different, concentrating more narrowly on the defence of professional boundaries and the right of the social worker to ply his trade.

33 But not for want of exhortation. Thus Barbara Castle, Opposition spokesman on social services, said at the annual study conference of the BASW: 'You cannot have effective caring services without a caring public opinion mobilised by an effective caring government. In your own professional interest you must get into the political fight because that is where

---

the fight for resources is' (reported in *The Times*, 28 October 1972). The main point to be made here is that Mrs Castle has shown the way which professional and political concerns may be accommodated under the same rubric.

34 H. J. Ehrlich, 'Notes From a Radical Social Scientist: February 1970', in J. D. Colfax and J. L. Roach (eds), *Radical Sociology*, Basic Books, 1971.

4

The politics of uncertainty: a study in the socialization of the social worker

Geoffrey Pearson

The 'radicalism' which is in the air in social welfare does not always look like the social worker's friend: it would not be going too far to suggest that some social workers experience it as an assault. This paper examines the groundwork of this heated confrontation: it suggests an understanding of some aspects of the being and becoming of a social worker, and explores how the moral–political debate represents itself in his everyday professional life. It is an essay in the politics of the social worker's experience.

Joining the club

Getting at experience, and rendering experience intelligible, is not easy. We dress our experience in fine clothes to show it off; it is structured, and sometimes choked, by our language and culture in our efforts to make it accountable to others. One dimension of getting at experience is getting inside the skin of another language. Alfred Schütz observes: 'In order to command a language freely as a scheme of expression, one must have written love letters in it; one has to know how to pray and curse in it.'[1]

Language here might stand as a paradigm for skill-acquisition: there is more to learning a language than the technical matters of linguistic symbols (alphabet, vocabulary) and rules (spelling, grammar, syntax) for putting the symbols together. Elsewhere Schütz suggests:[2]

All possible communication presupposes a mutual tuning-in relationship between communicator and the addressee of the communication. This relationship is established by the reciprocal sharing of the Other's flux of experience in inner time, by living through a vivid present together, by experiencing this togetherness as a 'We'. Only within this experience does the Other's conduct become meaningful to the partner tuned in on him.... Communicating with one another presupposes, therefore, the simultaneous partaking of the partners in various dimensions of outer and inner time—in short growing old together.

Learning occupational skills and knowledge so that one 'belongs' thus involves an experiential dimension: a taking on of the badges, style, and slang of office. Education is not simply a process of learning something which one did not know before, but also of *becoming* someone whom one did not know before. Everett Hughes, attempting to describe the acquisition of a professional world view which involves relinquishing lay conceptions of what the profession is about, calls it 'a passing through the mirror so that one looks out on the world from behind it ... [creating] a sense of seeing the world in reverse'.[3]

Perhaps Hughes overestimates the *completeness* of this transition. Nevertheless, these hardly describable qualities lie as a gulf not only between the 'lay' world and the 'professional' world, but also between differently constructed worlds of different occupations with different tasks at hand. Thus, in arriving at an understanding of an occupational grouping and its ways of doing things, the negotiation between the differently-mirrored world of the social worker, say, and the social scientist is crucial: fundamentally, one must look at the occupation either from the inside, as it were, or from the outside. On the one hand, a writer who finds, as Cohen describes it, that 'it is hard to describe ... techniques [of casework and group counselling] without making them sound like something out of Alice in Wonderland'[4] is in some difficulties. By standing outside the mirror he will be able to get a different hold on the social reality of the occupation than that which is professionally agreed and immediately accessible to the professionally socialized subject, but he will thereby find much of the richness and variation in that reality lost to him. On the other hand, 'going native' and attempting to elucidate professional culture from an insider perspective has its own problems. Professional culture, like any other, is not simply if at all instrumental. It does not necessarily face squarely, or contribute to the resolution of, problems which face the professional in his work. Especially in an occupation such as social work which involves as a day-by-day matter the juggling of elusive qualities and priorities of 'need', professional culture has the important function for professionals of offering ready-made, *routinized* 'solutions', as opposed to solutions which are *grounded* in the complex moral calculus of welfare services. To quote Schütz once more: 'It is the function of cultural patterns to eliminate troublesome inquiries by offering ready-made directions for use, to replace truth hard to obtain by comfortable truisms, and to substitute the self-explanatory for the questionable.'[5]

The danger for the man who would learn to 'pray and curse' in the language of another is that he might forget to write research reports in his own.[6] Difficult as these problems are in any social scientific enterprise, they are compounded where there is a shortage of boundary-markers between what constitutes 'social science', 'applied social science', and 'artful making-do' in practical matters of welfare. Researchers into welfare are thus likely to let what they do themselves colour what they see their subjects doing—when they can make that distinction at all easily—and where they cannot, they may force distinctions that are not always appropriate.

Moreover, the nature of welfare matters is such that common-sense attitudes will necessarily influence how we understand what is going on within the welfare professions. Freidson, commenting on research into medicine writes:[7]

[medicine] is all too often discussed by both physicians and laymen, and for that matter by social scientists in a spirit of positively mystical sentimentality. His spokesmen praise the physician for his superhuman qualities; his detractors damn him because he is not superhuman. The patient is defended as one of the poor, timid, Little People, oppressed by wicked, overbearing doctors; he is damned as an ignorant and wilfully destructive meddler in medical affairs.

Becker distinguishes two versions of such 'sentimentality': the conventional, and the unconventional. 'Conventional sentimentality' does not question the integrity of professionals, and takes as an assumptive underpinning to its inquiries the neutrality and impartiality of physicians, welfare officials, and police officers, etc. 'Unconventional sentimentality' makes different kinds of assumptions and takes for granted that the police are corrupt, physicians are case-hardened, money-grabbing sharks, whereas social workers are do-gooders, bent on their own moral salvation.

Now clearly these different 'sentimentalities' are not plucked out of the air; what they reflect, and what the research problem itself mirrors, are the kinds of meanings and values that can be attached to the field of welfare practice. Entering the profession of social work—joining the club—involves embracing some of these competing evaluations and eschewing others, and what we are interested in here is the extent to which the adoption of such a refined conception of his professional role furthers his professional practice. In particular, I want to pursue the relationship between this 'professionalism' and the radical critique of social work.

Fundamental to this critique is the rediscovery of social welfare as an activity which is grounded in moral–political choices. I can best illustrate this by reference to an early contribution of Kingsley Davis in which he points to the fact that the objectives of social welfare programmes might be appreciated in different ways by different parties; social welfare for him does not consist in the 'application' of science and technique to problems, but also involves the 'manipulation and adjustment of human values'.[8] Thus, the objectives of social work are *problematic*: 'It is not possible to take for granted a practical goal and work towards it.'[9] In brief, what one views as a 'problem', what one accepts as a 'solution' to that problem as defined, and what will be regarded as a satisfactory means (technique) for arriving at a given solution to a given problem is a matter of debate; it involves options about the kind of life-style one is prepared to tolerate, and will differ according to one's position in the social structure, and in particular, the social structure of the welfare enterprise. Enlarging on the number of parties which Davis represents in his own scheme, we can say that included in any list of those with some purchase on this definitional procedure will be client, client's family and kin, neighbourhood, various pressure groups, 'public opinion', professional opinion and expertise, and the considerations of the administrators of social service organizations, and elected representatives. 'Professional opinion' would include not only that of social workers, but also inter-professional conflicts and rivalries, for example, between prison officers and social workers on what to do about 'toughs', or between social workers and schoolteachers on what to do about truants. Furthermore, the professional will not always act 'in role': on occasions, 'good sense' will indicate something different from what might be generally understood as officially prescribed action.

Usually boiled down to a shorthand—'the individual versus society'—all of these are *legitimate* interests; indeed, how one would define the illegitimacy of interests would add a further equation to this moral–political calculus. This is, however, a deflating if not depressing perspective for the social work professional, for it is precisely because his expertise is routinized, and not morally grounded in the social reality of welfare, that he can lay claim to expertise. Skill in routine professionalism is the application of technique to problems where the nature of problem and solution is assumed. In social work, routine professionalism finds different modes of expression: 'I am a person who puts the client first'; 'I am a professional who knows what is good for people'; 'I am an official who implements organizational policies'; 'I am a therapist/expert in human relation who oils the works of an otherwise dehumanized organizational apparatus.' Nevertheless, it will be recognized that each of these modes represents only a *partial* expression of the total field of interests in social welfare. 'Radicalism' assaults the sensibilities of the professional because it de-routinizes, and points through routines to the moral dilemmas which lie behind them. It asks quite simply, 'What are social workers *really* doing?' and in so doing it joins arms with some versions of social science which, while they are not politically radical, are theoretically radical. Thus, radicalism points to *uncertainty*, and what I will now proceed to is an account of some aspects of the traditional professional socialization of social workers, and the extent to which it arms him against this moral abyss which, to put it lightly, would constitute a very busy professional day should its implications be taken seriously.

Value orientations in professional culture

In order to get quickly to the heart of the social work student's socialization and preparation for professional practice, I will focus on the value system elaborated within social work. Social work takes its professional code very seriously: it is a core component of educational programmes and theoretical texts, and part of the examinable syllabus for student recruits. It claims to identify 'what social work is about', and 'what social workers should do', and shapes the understanding of what kinds of decisions should be made within social work and what the nature of those decisions is. However, focusing on 'values' should not be taken as implying a theory of socialization as the internalization of norms: it is not my intention to suggest that social work students swallow the rule-book and reproduce it in action. The sense of 'socialization' which lies at the back of my remarks is one which understands professional culture as providing a 'language' (concepts, imagery, devices, recipes) for grasping reality and processing it. Nevertheless, in so far as social work's value system is developed and employed professionally in such a way as to suggest that it does provide guides to action, I will explore the basis of such claims, but find them groundless. The dominant imagery of the value code socializes for inaction; the professional social worker, I will argue, is a professional ditherer.

Without engaging the complexity of the matter, there is general agreement that any systematic presentation of the value system would contain the following propositions:

1 The client has a right to expect that his communications should have a confidential status.

2 The client has the right to determine the course of his own actions (the principle of 'self-determination').

3 The client has the right not to be judged by the social worker (the 'non-judgmental' attitude).

4 The client should be regarded with warmth and positive feeling, whatever his actions. This, the difficult notion of 'acceptance', suggests the possibility of separating a man from his actions: 'Love the sinner, but hate the sin.'

5 Underlying all these is a general principle of 'individuation': each man is unique; all men have innate dignity and worth.

These values, which seem to offer clear directions for preferred courses of action, have been understood in different ways at different times. One possible scheme of interpretation is to view the value system as a set of subsidiary statements which issue from the core sentiment of 'individuation'. As a scheme which might offer grounds for action I will dismiss this quickly, although with an important reservation: while this global value commitment could stand as a defiant statement of human dignity, it hangs in the air with no indication of how one might realize the commitment in practice. We can agree with Rein that, 'unless its implications and consequences are drawn for professional practice, it is not a useful frame for action'.[10] Indeed, it is an abstract and debilitating creed, filling student social workers with high ambitions, but no indication of where to go with them; a pseudo-militancy which leads easily to a sense of futility.

A second option is to regard the value system as a prescriptive code relating to client–worker transactions, delimiting the activity and obligations of the worker, and stating the right and obligations of the client. It could be seen as an expression of the qualities of professional service which Parsons terms 'universalistic, functionally specific, and affectively neutral'.[11] A closer examination reveals, however, that the value system is a somewhat one-edged account of the professional–client bargain. Compare the occupational activity of salespeople: a salesgirl at a counter, for example, will have a 'professional code', however poorly articulated, which will indicate not only the rights of clients to equal service regardless of class, race, appearance, etc., but also what client behaviour will limit and signal an end to 'professional' obligations. We might list here the use of abusive language, attempts to interfere with other customers' purchases, passing dud cheques, 'getting fresh', etc. Now, while the social work ethic gives a more elaborate account of client *rights*, it gives only the poorest indication of the other side of the equation (i.e., that client rights are limited): the social worker's ethic, in theory, offers a *limitless* relationship, although in practice, of course, the social worker is able to offer no such thing. For the social worker is an official of a bureaucratic organization, as well as a person engaged in a 'relationship'. In summary, as a code for professional transactions, social work's value system neglects any account of office: the exercise of power in the client–worker relationship is never made explicitly problematic, except in a truncated form as 'authority', and the social worker is left without bearings in this area.

Moreover, even as a code of client *rights* the ethic is inadequate. Both in practice and in theoretical accounts of the ethic, the system of rights is infringed and compromised. Clients only have a right to 'self-determination' where it does not lead to infringements of others' 'rights to self-determination' or to 'foolish' actions; some client behaviour is 'judged'; and the right to confidentiality is not absolute, and is on occasions openly abused. Similarly, in relation to the notion of 'acceptance', it is no idle remark of Timms that it contains an 'in spite of it all' element: ' "Accepting" seems to contain some hidden reference to that *which might prevent* something being accepted' [My italics].[12]

These ambiguities and infringements of the professional code cannot simply be dismissed as 'bad practice'. The requirements of office and organizational procedure point to a system of *hidden* rules operating against the acknowledged ethical framework; if social work is anything it is an organizationally grounded practice, and social work's ethic is but one side of an incomplete equation.

A third, and final, interpretive scheme to be considered here is the idea of the value system as a disguised system of technical rules for effecting change in client behaviour. Thus, it is a feature of social work's professional code that it is worn very much on the sleeve, and is quite central to the whole enterprise. It would not surprise us, I think, if a physician were to commit gross breaches of his official ethical code if he believed his actions were in the interests of his patient. Indeed, in his *Profession of Medicine* Freidson goes so far as to suggest that in medicine, 'the customary professional characterization of the client ... insists on his ignorance and irrationality'.[13] Perhaps if he is only concerned about the eventual possibility of giving the patient an injection, the physician can afford to connive or bully. The social worker's client, on the other hand, is unlikely to respond favourably to being pushed around; unlikely to be able to judge alternatives open to him if he is constantly criticized for 'false moves'. Within this framework the *ethics* has transformed itself into *techniques* of how to secure client change or 'growth', and how to facilitate constructive problem-solving activity.

Here is perhaps the formulation which provides the most solid set of references between the 'values' and an action scheme. The principles of confidentiality, self-determination, non-judgmentality, acceptance, etc. fall easily into place as techniques to facilitate required client action without fragmenting into argument, defensive justification, or fear. The core notion of 'individuation' stands as a reminder to 'start where the client is', guarding against stereotyping, routine work, etc. The techniques which the values embody, however, are those of a psychodynamic psychotherapy, and the action guides hold only so long as psychoanalysis is accepted as the paradigm for professional conduct. The unwritten history of social work would probably reveal that where there has been no psychoanalytical hegemony, pushing clients around 'for their own good', bullying, scaring, arm-twisting, conning, and putting to shame have all been considered worthy elements in the noble pursuit of helping people to help themselves.[14]

A commonsense resilience in social work, moreover, grounded in the practical organization of day-to-day work, protests against the idea that social work is psychotherapy. The interpretive scheme of values-as-techniques comes away in the hand, and leaves the social worker once more without a map for action. In its most everyday formulation, the principles of social work, given organizational requirements, are 'impractical' and 'unrealistic'.

Action and audience: structured uncertainty

If the values of social work can be said to constitute 'rules' which might act as guides to professional action, then it is clear that these rules are frequently violated and compromised, and that they compete with a hidden set of rules which, while they have considerable weight in determining professional action, are not given voice in the professional creed. The commonly funded knowledge of social work will tell us that compromise stems from the rough and tumble of the social worker's day, heavy caseloads, office routine, administrative requirements, and the mundane business of 'getting the job done'. We can bunch these together under the heading of 'commonsense' rules, although this is clearly unsatisfactory since, apart from telling us that the professional code of social work is not 'commonsense', it gives no clearer hold on what 'proper' professional conduct might be. What I wish to suggest, however, is that violations of the professional code have a systematic and patterned character. To propose the antinomies to the value system as I have framed it:

1 The client's communications to officials of a public service, involving as they do matters of public money, and in the last analysis public order, have the character of public knowledge.

2 The client's actions, impinging on the rights of others and on the obligations and priorities of public service, are not free.

3 The client's actions, by their nature problematic to 'consensus', are judged.

4 The client's rights as citizen do not entitle him to anticipate that regardless of any act on his part he will continue to be 'accepted': he can, in short, be 'outlawed'.

5 Clients, as the objects of a large-scale organization with many bureaucratic features, will be treated within an administrative machinery as *cyphers*.

If these are taken, whatever their merits as a guiding moral philosophy, as the competing rule-set which interferes with the unlicensed operation of the social worker's professional code, then we can see that the violations of this code are generated from the classical problem in the political theory of civil society: in its most abstract expression, the relationship of individual (subject) to order (Leviathan). The day-to-day problems facing the social worker in the implementation of his moral code thus emerge as the superficial appearance of a powerful and embracing value dilemma: how, in a conundrum devised by Ernest Becker, to have a 'community of privacy'.[15] What the difficulties of the professional code express is not a value *commitment* to some preferred course of action, so much as a value *problem*.

The social worker's client, although he may be depicted as such in the abstract professional code, is not a citizen with full 'credentials'. He does not play an effortless part in the daily business of civil life. In commonsense public imagery he is the deviant, the inadequate, the misfit, the outcast: he is strayed from the path ('deviant', from the root *de via*); an inept performer of the cultural scripts who has not learned his lines; one who does not fit in with 'the way of things'; he is outlawed and cast out from the centre of operations. Although challenged in recent years by client organizations such as Claimants' Unions, Preservation of the Rights of Prisoners (PROP), or the Mental Patients' Liberation Front, the idea of his defending his rights is ludicrous if not offensive; the idea of his asserting his common humanity, impudent. In all cases, he is *by definition* what is outside, alien to, and other than the normal process of the body politic. Decidedly out of things, he can only appear to members as *un-natural* and other worldly. Outside of culture, he is not to be comprehended, but only to be explained. More object than subject, monster rather than actor, he is not afforded the rationality which is assumed to be an underpinning of politics and access to political process. The relations of members with 'full credentials' to the deviant are uneasy: unable to mask the purely private in his make-up, he floods the social scene with unwarranted privatizations; or he unnerves us by being indifferent about everything which he should cherish; or, again, his contribution to the social bargain is so shadowy and unconvincing that our own actions are plagued by indecision. He disrupts the joy of flawless social intercourse.

Thus, the 'shirker' is someone who has recognized what one is not supposed to recognize—that work can be less privately meaningful than welfare benefits—if the show is to go on. Similarly, the client who quite simply cannot fit in with the demands of the administrative machinery of the social services brings to our awareness the violence done to the lives of many people in their efforts to fulfil their part as uncomplaining clients in the sacred bargain by which we convince ourselves that we live in civilized times that care for the sick, the poor, and the needy.

From another vantage point it is possible to grasp further dimensions of the delicate fabric of this interface between 'individual' and 'society'. The line between what we call 'help' and what we call 'interference' is a difficult one to draw. Some helpers are seen as meddlers; others as case-hardened entrepreneurs; some as saintly givers of the gifts of light and air; others as 'do-gooders' bent on moral conversion and the improvement of their own soul. The state of affairs which defines a chat about child management with a physician as 'psychotherapy', while the same conversation with 'the man from the welfare' becomes a case of 'State interference', the infringement of privacy, or the reckless meddlings of some do-gooder, is as important as it is curious. Social welfare exists on the hinge of this paradox. An old lady asking to be admitted to a residential home will be looking for help, and she will sometimes complain that the home is regimented and not geared to individual needs; and, as often as not, she will be right. Should a member of staff conduct an 'intake interview' in order to get to know her a little better, assess the possibilities of catering to her individual needs, and monitor provisions against the experience of clientele, she may well complain—as will her relatives and neighbours—that this is an infringement of her liberty and privacy. And again, in a sense, they will be right. Social work attempts to occupy the middle ground which this old lady represents, and often the middle ground does not exist.

Client and social worker thus act out the paradoxical drama of our sociality. The response within professional culture is twofold. On the one hand, a distinction is made between practice which is client-oriented and 'professional' and practice which is rule-following and 'unprofessional' : the dilemma is represented as an *opposition* between what is social work and what is *not* social work. Here I am arguing that professional social work, as we have understood it, *is* that opposition. On the other hand, the dilemma—and with it all of Hobbes, Kant, Spinoza, Rousseau, etc.—is boiled down to a soapy professional catechism : 'Social work has the dual obligation to man *and* society.' How, we may ask, does this core aspect of the imagery of professional culture prepare the student for social work practice?

Essentially, social work's value system, as a scheme for action, is *empty*. Here, in the use of 'emptiness', I follow Reiff's depiction of the admittedly quite different moral impulse of Freud's psychoanalysis. Characterizing Freud's moral imperative as an 'ethics of honesty', requiring a disclosure and overhauling of false motives by the technique of 'ruthless talk', he writes: [16]

> Honesty has no content. Though the Freudian training involves
> intellectual judgement ... based on calm and neutral appraisal of
> all the demanding elements of a life-situation, still, the freedom
> to choose must end in choice. Here, at the critical moment,
> the Freudian ethic of honesty ceases to be helpful.
>
> Being honest, admitting one's nature, does not resolve specific
> issues of choice. The Freudian ethic emphasizes freedom at
> the expense of choice. To achieve greater balance within the
> psyche, to shift the relative weights of instinct and repression,
> installs no new substantive rules of decision.

Social work's value code delineates the core value problem of the helping act as the regulation of the transactions of 'individual' and 'society' (and here again I employ a shorthand expression for the politicking of various interests, parties, and groupings with each other) but does not suggest *how* they are to be regulated. The dominance of the 'individuation' clause in the code suggests, of course, that decisions will be made on the 'merits of the individual case': but, how is one to judge the merits of the case without a general guiding framework? Eschewing any unitary guiding scheme which would thrust him into value *commitment*, the professional social worker suffers, as C. Wright Mills put the matter, from 'an occupationally trained incapacity to rise above a series of "cases" '.[17]

By what rules, then, must the social work student learn to judge his performance 'professional'? For any matter of performance audience is crucial : as one Russian author is said to have remarked, 'You can go mad at the mere thought of being read.'[18] Different performances have different relations to their relevant audiences.

The comedian, for example, is pinned to his: laughter is the acid test of performance, and the separation of comedian from audience through the mass media, as Colin Fletcher has suggested, requires a re-definition of performance and role.[19] McHugh's study of the professional stage actor suggests a similar set of problems with different resolutions.[20] The stage actor, McHugh argues, is without a reliable set of rules to direct performance and, similarly to the comedian, he only knows that what he has done is effective when the audience loves it. There may be rules, perhaps, by which to act, but no rules by which to judge that a particular piece of rule-governed acting will meet the criteria of success. Faced with this intolerable uncertainty, the actor makes do by 'refusing to act in terms of public acclaim'[21] and by constructing an attitude of collegiality ('all actors are equal in competence') he dissolves the audience's power. Audiences are deemed incompetent to judge good acting. For the professional actor, therefore, collegiality resolves uncertainty by ignoring its effects.[22]

The structured uncertainty of the social worker's professional world is even more complete. At even the most basic level of performance—immediate client response—he is without firm guides. He cannot say confidently that if he does A he will 'cause' B to follow. This is what we mean when we say that his technical equipment is poorly grounded empirically. More crucially, however, at the level of providing 'solutions' to 'problems'—eventual 'effectiveness', rather than simple 'effect' (in the form of immediate client response)—rules are once more problematic. Matters are confounded, moreover, on recognition that—already lacking causal rules by which to judge effect (B follows A), and lacking evaluative rules by which to judge effectiveness—for the social worker, unlike the stage actor, the audience criterion also becomes problematic. The social worker is left asking by whose response, and by the solution of whose problems—client, employing agency, public, professional colleagues—is one to calculate effectiveness? The rules of his trade give him no guidance. It is little wonder that the social worker is tempted to resort to 'rule of thumb' when all that the formal component of his professional education indicates is: 'Here is the problem, get on with it.'

Images of organization in professional culture

I began with an account of the routine aspects of professional culture and its de-routinization by 'radical' critics. What can now be grasped is that this radical critique does not *invent* moral dilemmas: the conflicts and uncertainties to which it points are already embodied in the operations of the professional code.

Radicalism, while it may not help, certainly does not harm. We must therefore ask why it is that this radicalism can appear to the social worker as such an affront, and how the moral–political dilemmas have been resolved by routine within professional culture. Our discussion of the role of comedian and actor perhaps suggest modes whereby the social worker resolves the structured uncertainty of his professional world : by following bureaucratic rules; in the mystique of 'expertise' which can only be judged from within a closed order; by 'pleasing clients'; or by rule of thumb. These are all possible strategies open to the social worker, but I will leave to one side the empirical matter of their use in order to develop one more dominant theme of professional socialization, namely the place of organization in routine professional culture. Within the relationship of professional and organization are embedded all the threads of moral dilemma.

Historically, casework has achieved dominance in the field of social work. Its response to the moral–political dilemmas which I have explored here has been, in a phrase, to wish them away. Within the casework paradigm the central elements of social work are a worker who is a professional helper, a client who has sought help with a personal problem, and an activity which takes place between them (usually conceived of as a conversation) in an office, hopefully at a pre-arranged time. Divergences from this model are understood as 'the problems of the field' which will no longer exist in some heavenly future where there are enough social workers, offices, chairs, telephones, etc. to make caseloads 'manageable' and render the ideal of the 'casework relationship' realizable. The function of such myths, which have more than a superficial resemblance to cargo cults, remains unexamined in social work education. The effect of this professionally agreed 'knowledge', however, which is grounded in distinct organizational frameworks (particularly, American family casework agencies) is to perpetuate an unproblematic sense of professionalism, professional–client relationships, and, in particular, the relationship of professional to organization and welfare programme.

This is not to suggest that within the casework paradigm the organization is seen as something entirely in accord with professional enterprise: on the contrary, the professional ideology is essentially a liberal one where paymasters are 'ill-informed' and sometimes not even well-intentioned. Moreover, the organization is often conceived of as a fearsome thing, hostile to proper professional practice. However, the implications of this for immediate practice, as opposed to long-term policy reform, are poorly articulated. Equally, while it is allowed that client and worker may sometimes have different definitions of their joint enterprise, this is a world free of differentials in the power to make one's definitions stick.[23] Where any antagonism of interest is allowed within this paradigm, client and worker are 'on the same side': this is a model of professionalism which seems unable to conceive of itself as anything other than beneficent. Within its boundaries the social worker is always an unambiguous *helper*.

It is useful here to compare the functions of the psychiatrist. Thomas Szasz, commenting on the role of the psychiatrist in decisions concerning competence to stand trial, suggests that 'helpers' cannot help everyone:[24]

> It is comfortable to hold the simple view that physicians always try to help people, or at least never deliberately try to harm them. Unfortunately this is not so. It cannot be so. Modern society is a complex web of social relationships in which individuals and groups are in constant conflict. When physicians become entangled in such conflicts, they are bound to help some and harm others. I do not deplore the existence of this fact, but only its denial—especially when such denial serves strategic aims in an antagonistic relationship.

Szasz argues that it would be more proper for the psychiatrist to ground his conduct in an open recognition of the possibility of such conflicts. Indeed, he suggests that on some occasions it is more proper for the psychiatrist openly to act as his patient's adversary, and that in openly acknowledging the disjunction of his patient's interests and his own, he might even thereby be *more* helpful:[25]

> If what is wanted is an adversary proceeding better suited for repressing 'deviants'—whoever they might be—the thing to do is to have an adversary proceeding that is *not* an adversary proceeding.... The trouble with frankly recognising that a situation is adversary in character is that it helps the weaker party—the accused, the mentally ill, the socially oppressed—to defend himself.

An interesting short account of an adversary concept applied to the education of oppressed minorities, or people of a different cultural system, is provided by Wolcott in a paper entitled 'The Teacher as an Enemy'.[26] Writing of his experiences as a teacher in a Kwakiutl village school he says: 'What my pupils wanted most to get out of school was to get out of school.'[27] Wolcott draws some implications from what he calls an 'enemy perspective' of education: (1) the teacher can imagine how pupils feel towards him as a member of a conquering people and will not be overcome by feelings of *personal* inadequacy; (2) the teacher acknowledges systematic differences of life-style and value-orientation; (3) the teacher recognizes the 'existential plight' of pupils, namely that accepting his teaching might mean 'selling out, defecting, turning traitor'; (4) finally, he writes:[28]

> Few demands are made of enemy prisoners. Any demands are made explicitly; they are not based on assumptions of fair play, individual rights, ultimate purposes, or the dignity of office. . . . The perspective . . . invites teachers to examine the kinds of *differences* cherished by enemies just as they have in the past addressed themselves, at least ritually, to what they and their pupils share in common.

The adversary logic expressed by Szasz and Wolcott is not out of place in the field of social work: a client's characterization of a probation officer, for example, as a 'copper's nark', while it may not be charitable to his intent, has a certain cogency, given the structural location of the probation officer in criminal matters. Here I will pursue my argument by means of an example:

> Susan A. is a student placed for fieldwork practice in a Social Service Department. Her supervisor has allocated her a case which arose out of court proceedings over an issue of alleged child neglect; the outcome of the court hearing, which the parents understood could have resulted in their child being taken into the care of the Local Authority, was to recommend that the Social Service Department supervise the conduct of the parents. During subsequent home visits the student was given a cool reception. She was shown the child, the child's bedroom and the bathroom, and given a factual account of the family's conduct, and their interest in keeping out of trouble. She was told, 'We know why you're here—you're the Court Inspector.' The father was at times quite hostile and could see no point in having a 'friendly chat'. Susan felt that in the circumstances there was little more she could do than visit in a regular, perfunctory manner. Her supervisor told her that she was the receptacle of 'angry, hostile feelings', and that her main casework objective should be, 'to help the parents perceive you as a caring person in a helping role'.

The case is not atypical, and my point is not to argue whether Susan A. was receiving 'bad' supervision. It seems reasonable to suggest, however, that the parents' definition of the social reality of the social worker's role was just as valid as, if not more accurate than, that of the supervisor.

Systematically, the dominant paradigm of professional action and authority within social work generates this problem. It is unable

59

to yield a coherent scheme which can incorporate the possibilities that organizational programmes might be inadequate, or even hostile, to the client's needs. Nor is it mindful of the possibility that the relationship of client and worker might be that of adversaries. Again, not untypically, the supervisor's feelings in the above case were that the student's sense of hopelessness indicated a poor adaptation on her part to 'reality' and 'authority', and were symptoms of professional and personal immaturity.

Scott, in his study of professionals in welfare bureaucracies, writes: [29]

> Disciplined conformity to authority was regarded as a sign of maturity. As one supervisor explained to a recalcitrant worker, 'Maturity is involved in working with existing authority and in accepting it.' Another phrase often used to justify working within agency policy was that to do so was to 'accept the reality factors in the situation'. To resist agency policy was considered unrealistic and a waste of energies which could be devoted to constructive work.

Discussing the management of antagonisms between client, worker and organization in the supervisory relationship, Scott continues: [30]

> The professional reconciliation to such [adversary] policies was to de-emphasize the punitive character of the action and emphasize its protective nature. The worker's attention was focused on the party most likely to benefit from the action rather than on the party whose interests might be injured.... Supervisors using this approach did not appeal to the virtues of self-discipline and conformity for its own sake but faced up to the content of the particular policy and attempted to defend it as being fundamentally consistent with social work values and the best interests of clients.

What I am suggesting is that within the narrow sense of professionalism with which social work has provided itself, the worker is seen only as an unambiguous helper, and that there are various strategies for defending this view; where he does not help, it is because the worker has insufficient skill or experience. This professional representation of the work scene provides a powerful guiding imagery for both students and teachers of social work; but it is a *routine* solution to the task at hand, and it glides through the thorny moral and political dilemmas of organizational policy. In one essentially liberal statement of the aims and methods of field-work supervision for beginning students we read, for example: [31]

Young students are usually more mature intellectually than emotionally, and it is not the function of supervision to put old heads on young shoulders; the supervisor should therefore be prepared to accept that problems in relation to authority are to be expected, and that intellect may be used as a defence against feelings of inadequacy in the face of acute social problems. It is a function of university education to develop the student's critical faculties, and it is appropriate therefore in supervision to expect and accept criticism of the agency's work, ensuring only that this criticism is positive in intention and based on accurate and valid observation.

The need to caution fieldwork teachers to 'expect and accept' criticism of agency policy from students should not pass unnoticed: it alerts us to the fact that one should not anticipate this as a matter of course within the dominant image of professionalism. The statement itself, moreover, betrays core features of professional ideology. Through subtle shifts of meaning an equation is drawn between organizational efficacy, the ability to accept 'authority' and 'reality', and finally personal *immaturity*. The relationship of office and organization to need is thus redrawn as the problem of 'authority', and criticism of it is to be understood in terms of the student's personality and educational background; the statement reflects the tendency within the casework paradigm to reduce organizational–structural problems (the inability to meet client need) to an assumed personal failing on the part of students. Nor should it escape our attention that an alternative, but currently less fashionable, belief that social work organizations are too soft with clients would suffer a similar fate. This is not to suggest, of course, that students (and their more mature colleagues) will not *feel* impotent and inadequate in the face of distressing problems. The point at which such feelings become mobilized, however, will often be *where the organization is inadequate*, precisely the point at which 'intellectual'—and even downright 'negative' and 'emotional' —criticism becomes appropriate. However, professional culture masks the disjunction of organizational creed (what an organization says it is doing) and organizational effect (what an organization is actually doing), presenting criticism of this disjunction as an emotional 'defence' against 'powerful feelings'.

The image of organizational problems in professional culture can be summarized briefly. The policy of welfare organizations is no straightforward professional–technical matter: social welfare matters, impinging as they do on conceptions of the proper and responsible way to live, are subject to different interpretations which are played out in a wider debate of cultural, moral and political beliefs. The professional recruit, however, is denied access to this debate.[32] Antagonism between his belief system and established welfare practice is redefined in the professional world as an antagonism between himself and his supervisor's 'authority': the professional paradigm reproduces its more global reduction of organizational and social–structural issues to personal troubles and quirks in the microcosm of its educational practice.

'Radicalism' and 'professionalism'

There can be no doubt that this dominant paradigm of professionalism is breaking up. Social workers increasingly, it seems, come to view as legitimate enterprises matters of welfare rights, policy formulation, client organizations of the trade-union type, and conflict strategies. And yet, at the same time, there is abroad a sense of gloom and dejection: where to turn, what to do, how to help? Frequently one hears rumours—and admittedly, they are only rumours—of epidemics of depression on professional training courses in the face of what is understood as 'radical' criticism. Munday, for example, writes in hair-raising language about student recruits being exposed to 'general attacks on traditional beliefs in society ... assailed by a variety of academic material that is threatening, undermining and often downright depressing'.[33] Elsewhere, in an editorial to the British Journal of Social Work, Olive Stevenson writes that, 'social work has been having a hard time recently', and goes on to claim that some critics have based their criticism on 'wilful misrepresentation'.[34] The imagery of debate is not infrequently violent. Elizabeth Irvine describes social work as a 'battlefield', and talks of 'take-over bids' in social work education by ideologues:[35]

> Those who want to indoctrinate students against 'the ideology of social work' have three years to do it in before the graduate decides to enrol for professional training. Having made this choice, he remains free to discuss ideological issues ... but there is much else to be learned, and all too little time to learn it in. We can't discuss ideologies for ever.

Invariably it is 'sociologists' who are seen as being in the forefront of this struggle, and yet there is a surprise in store. From the tone of Munday's contribution, which also points the finger clearly at 'sociology' which 'teaches that it is our system which is at fault', thus reinforcing the beliefs of students who are 'highly motivated by very left-wing values',[36] one might imagine that he had some version of a marxist sociology in mind which would overthrow the state apparatus, and social work with it. But no:

when he gets down to naming names, Munday writes that he has in mind 'writers like Matza, Becker, and Cicourel [whose ideas] are intellectually fascinating and persuasive, but quite ominous for the social worker'.[37]

There is evidently something fishy here, and the more one looks at it, the fishier it gets. Matza, for example, as part of his pursuit of a 'naturalism' which remains true to the phenomena under study proposes in opposition to 'correctional' research methodology the stance of 'appreciation' which, on the face of it, is not unlike the social worker's attitude of 'starting where the client is'.[38] Howard Becker, labelling theorist, leans in sympathy with the underdog,[39] something not unknown within social work, while Cicourel offers accounts of the organizational definition of 'cases' which give elaborate justification to the cautionary notes in any casework text on the dangers of allowing preconceptions to colour the process of 'study–diagnosis–treatment'. Munday's list could be extended: it would include Lemert, Goffman, Berger, Kitsuse, Scott, probably Garfinkel, and certainly Jack Douglas—all of them no more than liberal in their approach, and some members of the 'radical right'. What is seen in the writings of these authors by Munday and others as ominous and subversive of professional endeavour is not a subversive politics of the left—although it is often taken as such by both detractors and devotees—but simply a unifying concern to make apparent the routine grounds of decision-making in welfare bureaucracies and the role of professional ideologies in determining imagery and official rates of deviance. To repeat: there is no more here than one would expect to find in the average casework text, but what *hurts* is that the moral and organizational grounds of routine professionalism are rendered explicit. In the light of these accounts, what stands apparent is that which has been wished away in the traditions of routine welfare professionalism: here is a 'return of the repressed'.[40]

I have argued that the fear and confusion which social workers experience in the face of the radical critique of welfare flows from the de-routinization of its professional culture in that critique. One should not be surprised at the response. To be socialized means to take one's conception of the world for granted, and a feature of the taken-for-granted world is its objective and anonymous (absolute) character.[41] A threat to one's culture is literally a life-and-death matter; there is the truly ominous possibility that one might become bogged down in inaction. The radical critique of welfare is truly radical: it gets down to the *roots*, and rediscovers the world as a morally constructed world. It asks the social worker professional questions which in terms of his *routine* professionalism, by definition, he cannot answer.

Social work is surely among other things an application of social science, although I have given no indication of how the social worker might 'apply' it. One must remember also that the social scientist is himself a *professionally socialized social scientist*, and that his own taken-for-granted world stands in a tensional relationship to social welfare concerns on such highly charged matters as 'objectivity', 'value freedom', and the axis of 'theory-practice'. Sometimes the heated debate of the critique of welfare has not encouraged its easy reception within social work; sometimes, perhaps, the social scientist has forgotten himself in his attempts to hold on to his own professional world. These remarks are not intended, however, as a 'soft soap' conclusion which will lull the social worker back into his professional slumbers; I do not intend to reach for a consensus which I can hardly define. There is a cloying undergrowth of professional mythology in social work, and sometimes it is necessary to be *savage* in order to hack a way through it, and to cut oneself loose from one's own professional socialization. And if the debate is to *mean* anything, it is here that one must begin: in a redefinition of the grounds and objectives of professional social work education. Admittedly, attitudes and perspectives on professionalism will also be forcibly shaped and changed in the work situation after formal professional education has ended. Nevertheless, the socialization of the naïve recruit provides the backcloth—the imagery and recipes—against which, and out of which, to fashion critical professional self-conceptions.

We do our students a disservice when we cling to the idea of social work as a *unitary* profession. Social work is a highly *segmented* profession; there are many legitimate positions which can be adopted within it. As Bucher and Strauss suggest in their notion of a 'segmented' occupation, it is possible to disagree even as to what its core practices are, and still remain a 'member'.[42] One need not agree with a client who insists that he should be given what he *wants* rather than what, in professional judgment, he 'needs', in order to see that it is a position with moral grounds within the complex web of welfare; one need not agree with a lobby to 'bring back the birch' to see that it is a legitimate interest within the field *as defined*. To begin to ground social work education in such dilemmas would be to suggest a radically different conception of 'profession' to that currently employed.

There are no easy victories to be won here, but if one cannot give answers, one can at least ask questions. The interpenetrations of professionalism, power, interest, conflict, morality and economy within social work require themselves to be fought out at both the highest theoretical level, and at the everyday level of mundane practice; both in the realm of abstraction, and in that of technology.

But professions do not take on such tasks easily. 'Professionalism' does not have to do with grasping a wide conception of the place of oneself and one's work in the world; it does not involve grasping oneself *reflexively*. It means learning the catechisms of a closed order; it means the narrowing of grasp and manner, withdrawing into a shell. This is not simply a problem for social work, but reflects the way in which we conceive of the growth and organization of our whole social life. The word 'professional' means a commitment to an order. Only in our idiom does it assume the meaning of 'acting responsibly'. Then in what sense can social work be a 'profession'?

A professionalism which closes itself off is, for social welfare, death: social welfare is the negotiation of need and priority, and unless all social welfare programmes are bureaucratized and officials can scrutinize 'need' in the way that a desk clerk might check a driving licence (unmindful of the possibility of forgery), it will involve such negotiations at the lowest levels as well as at the highest. How many social workers, for example, ignore the illegal fiddling of some of their clients against the Department of Health and Social Security, an organization which social workers surely see as being unkind to themselves as well as to their clients? How many probation officers turn a blind eye to the breaches of the probation order by offences of their clients? How many social workers simply do not care about the fact that a client earns a pound or so more than social security regulations permit by working behind a pub bar at night? These are questions to which we do not know the answers, and perhaps nothing more than discretion will prevent us from ever knowing. But our commonsense knowledge tells us, as insiders to the codes and signals of the profession, that the social worker sometimes serves the function of a Lilliputian Robin Hood who, if he is not actually robbing the rich to feed the poor, is aiding and abetting the offence.[43] And the 'industrial deviance' of social work is surely not to be written off as a characterological quirk of 'offenders', involving as it does complex moral calculation and choice.

Of course, to do these things slyly, to turn a blind eye here or there, without relating it firmly to the idea of one's professionalism is easy. But to incorporate that *into* one's professionalism? To build the moral commitments embodied in the industrial deviance of welfare *into* rules and guides for action is to suggest a conception of 'professional' which might be too hot to handle. And yet, this is the kind of question with which social work is faced by its radical critics: the politics of social work involves not only the moral crusades of policy reform, but also the day-to-day moral hustle of the social worker's professional life.

Conclusion

Social work is an extremely testing job. It requires the social worker to work within conditions of scarcity, and often in the face of the acute hardship and pain of his clients. It also requires him to work within a complex, and ambiguous, moral calculus of need and priority. The present essay indicates some of the ways in which the social worker's professional code dodges these moral–political issues.

The essay carries certain implications: unless the profession of social work, and its educational sector in particular, faces its moral and political ambiguities squarely, there can be little hope of transcending the professional uncertainty of the social worker. Some of the uncertainty of the social worker, it must be said, has to do with the commonplace uncertainties of meeting (and trying to help) distressed people. The fundamental core of social work's present crisis, however, is its political uncertainty: politics makes social work dizzy when it looks at itself.

Notes

1 A. Schütz, 'The Stranger', in *Collected Papers, II*, edited with an introduction by A. Broderson, The Hague, Martinus Nijhoff, 1964, p. 101.

2 A. Schütz, 'Making Music Together: A Study in Social Relationship', in op. cit., pp. 177-8.

3 E. C. Hughes, *Men and Their Work*, Free Press, Chicago, 1958, p. 119. See also, F. Davis, 'Professional Socialization as Subjective Experience: The Process of Doctrinal Conversion among Student Nurses', in H. S. Becker *et al.* (eds), *Institutions and the Person: Papers Presented to Everett C. Hughes*, Aldine, Chicago, 1968, pp. 235-51.

4 P. Cohen, 'Subcultural conflict and working class community', *Working Papers in Cultural Studies*, no. 2, 1972, pp. 5-51.

5 Schütz, 'The Stranger', p. 95.

6 For a vivid description of a social anthropologist being sucked into the world of his subject, see C. Castaneda, *The Teachings of Don Juan*, Penguin, Harmondsworth, 1972; *A Separate Reality*, Knopf, New York, 1971; and *Journey to Ixtlan*, Bodley Head, London, 1972.

7 E. Freidson, *Patients' Views of Medical Practice*, Russell Sage, New York, 1961, p. 20.

8 K. Davis, 'The application of science to personal relations: a critique of the family clinic idea', *American Sociological Review*, vol. 1, no. 2, 1936, pp. 236-47.

9 Ibid.

10 M. Rein, 'Social work in search of a radical profession', *Social Work*, vol. 15, no. 2, 1970, pp. 13-38.

11 T. Parsons, *The Social System*, Free Press, Chicago, 1951, p. 434.

12 N. Timms, *The Language of Social Casework*, Routledge & Kegan Paul, London, 1968, p. 39.

13 E. Freidson, *Profession of Medicine: A Study in the Sociology of Applied Knowledge*, Dodd, Mead and Co., New York, 1971, p. 353.

14 See, for example, M. Brown, 'A Review of Casework Methods', in E. Younghusband (ed), *New Developments in Casework*, Allen & Unwin, London, 1966, pp. 11-38.

15 E. Becker, *The Structure of Evil: An Essay in the Unification of the Science of Man*, Braziller, New York, 1968, *passim*.

16 P. Reiff, *Freud: The Mind of the Moralist*, Gollancz, London, 1959, p. 321.

17 C. W. Mills, 'The professional ideology of social pathologists', *American Journal of Sociology*, vol. 49, no. 2, 1943, p. 171.

18 Quoted in E. M. Cioran, 'Civilized man: a portrait', *Salmagundi*, no. 20, 1972, p. 116.

19 C. Fletcher, 'Fool or Funny Man: The Role of the Comedian', in *Beneath the Surface: An Account of Three Styles of Sociological Research*, Routledge & Kegan Paul, London, 1974.

20 P. McHugh, 'Structured Uncertainty and its Resolution: The Case of the Professional Actor', in S. C. Plog and R. B. Edgerton (eds), *Changing Perspectives in Mental Illness*, Holt, Rinehart & Winston, New York, 1969, pp. 539-55.

21 Ibid., p. 552.

22 Ibid., p. 555.

23 Compare the handling of power in two different accounts of the problem: J. E. Mayer and N. Timms, *The Client Speaks*, Routledge & Kegan Paul, London, 1970; and T. J. Scheff, 'Negotiating reality: notes on power in the assessment of responsibility', *Social Problems*, vol. 16, no. 1, 1968, pp. 3-17.

24 T. S. Szasz, *Psychiatric Justice*, Macmillan, New York, 1965, p. 56.

25 Ibid., p. 71.

26 H. F. Wolcott, 'The teacher as an enemy', *Practical Anthropology*, vol. 19, no. 5, 1972, pp. 226-30.

27 Ibid., p. 227.

28 Ibid., p. 230.

29 R. A. Scott, 'Professional Employees in a Bureaucratic Structure', in A. Etzioni (ed.), *The Semi-Professions and Their Organizations*, Free Press, New York, 1969, p. 117.

30 Ibid., pp. 120-21.

31 Joint University Council for Social and Public Administration, *Field Work in Social Administration Courses*; ed. E. E. Sainsbury, with a foreword by D. V. Donnison, National Council of Social Service, London, 1966, p. 36.

32 For an account of the relationship between recruit images of social work and professional ideology, see G. Pearson, 'Social work as the privatized solution of public ills', *British Journal of Social Work*, vol. 3, no. 2, 1973, pp. 209-27.

33 B. Munday, 'What is happening to social work students?', *Social Work Today*, vol. 3, no. 6, 1972, pp. 3-4.

34 Editorial, *British Journal of Social Work*, vol. 2, no. 1, 1972, p. 1.

35 E. Irvine, Letters, *Social Work Today*, vol. 3, no. 9, 1972, p. 22.

36 Ibid., pp. 3-4.

37 Ibid., p. 4.

38 D. Matza, *Becoming Deviant*, Prentice-Hall, Englewood Cliffs, 1969, ch. 2.

39 H. S. Becker, 'Whose side are we on?', *Social Problems*, vol. 14, 1967, pp. 239-47.

40 For a fuller account of the relationship of these versions of 'radical' social science and social welfare, see G. Pearson, 'Misfit Sociology and the

Politics of Socialization', in I. Taylor, P. Walton and J. Young (eds), *Critical Criminology*, Routledge & Kegan Paul, London, 1975, and G. Pearson, *The Deviant Imagination*, Macmillan, London, 1975.

41 A. Schütz, *Collected Papers, I*, edited with an introduction by M. Natanson, Martinus Nijhoff, The Hague, 1967, pp. 74ff.

42 R. Bucher and A. L. Strauss, 'Professions in process', *American Journal of Sociology*, vol. 66, no. 4, 1961, pp. 325-34.

43 For a different suggestion on the relationship between social work and banditry, see my 'Social work as the privatized solution ... op. cit. An extended account of research on this 'industrial deviance' is also to be found in G. Pearson, 'Making Social Workers: Bad Promises and Good Omens', in R. Bailey and M. Brake (eds), *Radical Social Work*, Edward Arnold, London, forthcoming.

5

Becoming a social worker

R. Deacon and M. Bartley

Social work training courses do not simply provide a setting where students may learn about the extent and history of the social services, about the nature, causes, and solutions of personal and social problems, or about the job they will be required to do when they are qualified. A social work training course is a setting in which students who come expecting to learn ways of remedying the social distress they see around them are socialised into becoming a certain type of professional person, taught to think in a particular way and to use an often confused collection of social work maxims, and come to accept, if often with cynical reservation, that they are members of a new profession. A social work course, in other words, involves not only the assimilation of 'facts and theories' for use in practice but also a process in which students learn to 'make out' as social workers.

Becoming a social worker means passing through a number of interrelated processes involving the action and reaction of tutor and taught. We would like to try and describe this process in some detail as a result of the research we undertook from September 1970 to July 1971 into part of a polytechnic's two-year child care officer training course as experienced by six students in their second year.

These six students spent all of their second year's practical placement, which occupied half of every week (the other half was spent in academic work) in a new unit attached to a settlement. One important aspect of their collective experience at this unit was their attachment in pairs and singly to various schools in the neighbourhood of the settlement where they were to 'identify needs ... and develop different ways of meeting those needs'. It was this aspect of their experience that we studied in depth by attending frequent meetings held at the settlement between the students and their supervisor, by interviewing participants in the project, by observing

69

in the schools involved, and by having access to the students' written material. Although the focus of the research was on the schools project as one aspect of their experience, our discussions with their supervisor and social work tutors, and our observation of social work courses in the college, enabled us to learn a lot about the applicability of what we observed in the schools project to social work education in general. The initial possibility that we would have been studying one rather special aspect of social work— community work—was avoided because the supervisor of the unit was a specialist in psychiatric social work, and valued casework as the primary form of social work intervention. The students in fact were unable effectively to initiate action which might have been considered as 'community work' because they had had no training in this area and there was little input of such theoretical or practical teaching either from the polytechnic or from the settlement during the period of their placement. In addition to our observation of this experimental field placement, we have, in building up our account of the process of becoming a social worker, drawn on our experience of attempting to teach sociology to social work students.

We have abstracted three distinct but related processes that social work students pass through in training. They involve: first, the discouragement of attempts to analyse critically the structures and institutions of society; second, the encouragement of intense personal evaluation of the student both by himself and his tutor and supervisor; third, the encouragement of students to adhere to a set of social work professional maxims which we believe we can show to be very confused. All these processes are underpinned by a general disavowal of intellectuality, of theoretical thinking, that we think characterises social work training. We describe these processes in more depth in the next sections. We then examine in general how we think students learn to 'make out' as social workers and then provide an account of the specific ways in which the students made out in the course we studied. We give an account of how the several processes operated in the school situation and the effect that they had on the students' learning and professional development. Finally, in the section on the politics of the placement we ask why this might be the case, and advance some general notions which also serve as an attempt to extend the interactionist perspective in sociology to include considerations of power relationships which must affect any social situation under study.

Although we abstract the three separate processes in the following sections, this cannot be done without damage to the complex whole. For this reason, readers will only grasp the totality and hence something of the reality of the situation by reading to the end.

The kind of things students did in their practical placements in the schools included running with selected children weekly groups, aimed at helping to solve children's social and educational problems, visiting parents to explain something of the work and purpose of the school, organising regular visits by boys to an old people's home, running in collaboration with the children, a survey of local attitudes towards the area and its social services.

A host of other ideas for action were thrown up especially in the early stages of the placement. One piece of work undertaken by all students was the mounting of a conference towards the end of the placement on the question of whether teachers should be social workers, which was attended by all the heads of the schools involved as well as other interested people.

In addition to the students' attachment to the schools a large part of their two-and-a-half day week spent at the settlement was concerned with other aspects of the placement not connected with the schools project such as managing a traditional small social work caseload.

Cooling out social structural criticism

An important aspect of social work training as we observed it is its ability to deflect students away from criticisms, which they might attempt to develop, of structures and institutions in society. Such critical awareness, though helping the student to understand the problems he has to deal with as a social worker, violates the strategic necessity of his college tutor and fieldwork supervisor to present an acceptable front to those in command of vital resources. This 'cooling out' is directly related to other processes described below, and is accomplished primarily by the channelling of social–structural or institutional criticism into psychologistic thinking. Our observations relate particularly to the way in which the students' view of the school structure, for example the power invested in head teachers or the class nature of education, is constrained.

The emphasis is placed on the psychological characteristics of headmasters, rather than the power invested in them by their institutional position and the effect this has on the education children receive. A second channelling mechanism can be seen in the way any insistence by the student on the criticism of institutions is taken as indicating something about the student rather than about the institution. The fact of offering such an unacceptable idea is seen as indicative of a need in the student to challenge authority. Thus one student, at an early group meeting, reacted to a suggestion that they had to tread lightly in the schools and gently increase understanding between social workers and teachers, by expressing a desire for more forthright action and saying that 'they ought to shoot headmasters who expel lads from school'. The practical work supervisor's response was 'You're feeling very angry about the general situation and transferring it to your particular situation. You don't want to be there—you're dissatisfied with yourself. Maybe you're angry that Jill has a foothold in the school and you don't.' Though obviously this is not always the case, the supervisor's denial here of the reality in the student's reaction does seem to do less than justice to the latter's remark—which has to be understood, of course, as a symbolical comment rather than a programme for action.

This aspect of the socialisation of social workers seems to result from the continuing domination of social work courses by a version of psychoanalytic thinking, which provides a set of maxims which can be used to explain and justify these channelling processes to, and later by, the student social worker. Sociology, where it is included is added on, not integrated into the teaching of social work method. Sociologists are often seen in the terms suggested above—their ideas and theories are disavowed in favour of a delving into why individual teachers need to be authoritarian, destructive, and dismissive of personal feelings.

We were offered an explanation of one of the principles that guide social work teaching by one of the social work tutors concerned. This explanation helped us to understand this tendency of social workers to think of everything—including social institutions —in psychological terms. 'One of the principles behind this [aspect of social work learning] is that of the transfer of learning from one situation to another. I had a strong hope that students would be able to transfer learning from, say, their own family experiences to the school. If they learn in a family, for example, what it means when there is a silence, and how to understand whether to break it or let it go on, they should be able to transfer this understanding to what happens in a school.... We don't yet know how far it is possible to do this transfer of learning.'

The assumption seems to be that all larger social groups and institutions are really just an extension of family relations—the transfer of learning is always from the individual case or the small group situation to larger social formations, never the other way round. The more complex theory required to explain the relationships of individuals and families to larger social and economic groupings is ignored. We examine this aspect in greater depth in a later section where we look in detail at what happened in the schools.

Evaluation of the student's personality

The student has to undergo a continual process of evaluation of his own personality, assisted by his tutors and supervisor. A particular sort of 'warm and accepting' person, who is willing to accept the tutor's and supervisor's view of him is preferred to the seemingly 'colder', 'intellectual' student, who prefers to maintain a more independent position. The aim is to get the tutors' and students' view of the latter's personality to agree by the end of the course. The ability of a student to look at himself in the same way as his tutor or supervisor is a mark of maturity. Disagreement is a mark of defensiveness and immaturity, and demonstrates a lack of insight. The tutor's view is final. The student who prefers to get on with the business of understanding and attempting to change society is seen as perhaps not the sort of person to be a social worker. Such a process, in which the social work supervisor's official position gives her the power to re-interpret the student's own view of his personality and feelings, tends to make students reluctant to engage in open conflict with the views held by the supervisors and tutors. The deflection of criticism of social institutions into analysis of the critic's personality which we described earlier is one result of this process.

One of the more insidious aspects of this process derives from the differential rate of socialisation of students. Those who conform to the required image early in the course join with the tutors and practical work supervisor in 'helping other students to evaluate themselves more correctly'. All of this tends to justify a failure to deal effectively with the injustices of the world outside.

Two students in particular came in for more than their share of such attention in the nine months of the school's placement. Both of them were students who were at one time or other more critical than the others of the limitations to the effectiveness of their intervention in the school setting. One of these—Laura—exemplifies many of the points we are trying to make, so it will be useful to describe her situation in more detail.

Laura was one of the most academically able students in her year. She was less willing to take on trust the generalisations presented as 'social work theory', and sophisticated enough to withstand, to some extent, the turning-back of her criticisms into symptoms of her own personality. The experience she and one other student had in the first few weeks after they entered their allocated school strengthened their critical attitude towards some aspects of social institutions. They came to feel that to have any meaningful effect upon the problems as they saw them, innovatory action would be necessary. Yet the headmistress of this school had formed the opinion at the outset that the social work students were only there to help her with remedial teaching (thus, incidentally, linking social with educational–remedial problems but seeing the remedy in yet more teaching within the existing structure).

Neither Laura nor her partner in the school, Felix, felt that this sort of activity could help to solve the problems. As Felix put it 'There's no point in working with remedials if they are still going to be labelled "remedial" after I leave.' The students tried to suggest other projects with a broader scope which they felt they might carry out. Among the suggested projects were: 'group sessions with troublesome girls', 'meeting with all staff involved in welfare —the head, deputy head, counsellor, housemothers, educational welfare officer and us—in order to discuss mutual problems'. Laura commented in a much later interview that she was 'more interested in a general discussion of the school structure and how this affected the welfare of the kids'. The headmistress was incensed by their temerity in wanting to go beyond her own understanding of their brief and withdrew from the experiment, leaving the two students without a school.

During a confused series of episodes after this, Laura finally left the project altogether at her request but with the encouragement of the practical work supervisor. The substantive facts related to the school—the headmistress's withdrawal and Laura's critical views of the educational system—mysteriously dissolved at this point in our records into the supervisor's criticism of Laura's manicuring her nails in a meeting, and the supervisor saying that Laura disagreed with the way she taught. The upshot, of course, was that Laura was seen by her supervisor as not being a good person to be a social worker. Her fellow students followed this up (in Laura's absence) by a string of pseudo-psychoanalytic interpretations of her actions, which led a visiting student to protest: 'But Laura is not a client.'

Some of the quotations below taken from the events surrounding this episode indicate the sorts of personality stereotypes expected in social work students and point to some of the pastiche of ideas that go to make up the conventional wisdom of what a social worker is. This second aspect we discuss in more detail in the next section.

'If Laura isn't able to deal with a situation such as St Thomas's [the school] perhaps she shouldn't be a social worker.'
'Laura stood out like a sore thumb—she didn't have any friends in college except Susan.'
'As a social worker you must take the middle road and you must compromise—Laura doesn't understand this.'

'Perhaps she went to too many cocktail parties and therefore couldn't devote all her energies to being a social worker.'
'St Thomas's was just her presenting problem. She was really angry at having to be with us. We are a sort of mediocre bunch.'

Thus the school problem is turned into a presenting problem for the 'real' personal difficulties. The students avoid the issue of whether Laura has been right or wrong about either the school or the supervisor's role—they simply do not discuss this. Two further quotations from her fellow students which again focus on Laura's failure to develop the 'right' personality traits needed in a professional social worker are; 'Perhaps Laura will be all right with her clients but she'll never be able to get on with her colleagues'; 'As a community worker she would probably be o.k.—on a political level.'

Laura's view of herself and of social work did not coincide with her supervisor's. Her fellow students, who sometimes found her views difficult to understand, eventually accepted the opinion of their official superior, the practical work supervisor, and co-operated in re-interpreting Laura's personality so that to them her 'failure' seemed 'inevitable' and 'perhaps a good thing'. To underline the arbitrariness of this personality judgment we might add that Laura has since received commendation from her supervisor in a subsequent placement, where a conflict between Laura's view of the needs of clients, and views acceptable to the agency, did not arise.

Ben, another student who at first made attempts to criticise the school system and to doubt the effectiveness of possible social work interventions, was very different from Laura. His criticisms came not so much from an intellectual appreciation of the situation, but from his own experience, and a feeling that there were some basic injustices in society which were being ignored. Ben was of working-class origin and admitted to being envious of people who 'read a lot'. During the course of the placement he had much of his instinctively hostile reaction to arbitrary authority counselled out of him, and, outwardly at least, changed his view of himself during emotionally intense sessions with his supervisor and with the group. By the end of the year he was able to comment on the conference on social work in schools, organised by the unit. 'It was good, we succeeded in getting a dialogue of one profession with another.' His successful assimilation of the professional ethos had neutralised his propensity for asking embarrassing questions about the aims and goals of the project.

The change in Ben was brought about towards the end of the placement when his irregular attendance at the Monday morning sessions, used to discuss the schools project, caused the other students to feel that this demonstrated a lack of commitment to them and to the group's functioning. This led to an examination in Ben's absence of his behaviour throughout the project, and at a later meeting the rest of the group confronted him, asking him to explain himself. This in turn led them to review what they saw as the important elements of the functioning of the student group: notably the degree to which individual students felt free to express their feelings towards each other. It seemed that the student group itself, rather than its possible educational functions in relation to activities in the schools, had become of prime significance to the students. Ben replied: 'It had not occurred to me that the emotional side of the group was so important. I thought Mondays was a practical thing.' He added, 'I don't take the point that all mature students have problems at home.' Further pressed on the matter of why he did not attend regularly the following exchange took place:

Ben   'I don't see the supervisor as an authority figure—that's why I never bother to explain why I'm not here.'
Another student 'You do have a difficulty about authority'
'Are you on good terms with your dad?'
(this student was the one who much earlier, before, as he said, he had 'learned to be diplomatic', wanted to shoot headmasters).

This type of session, of which there were more towards the end of the placement, and which showed Ben already learning his lesson, was punctuated by mutual 'reassurances' about how the students had got close enough to each other to tear 'each other's guts out' without 'destroying each other'. The achievement of this kind of personal contact was seen by all as an important part of becoming a social worker but the relationship of it to the practice of social work was never made clear—though the focus on explanation in terms of personality is obvious enough. ·

Acceptance of social work maxims

Channelling off what is seen as potentially dangerous criticism and counselling out 'undesirable personality traits', if they are to be successful must be accompanied by the presentation of some positive ideas to adhere to. This is achieved by the complex of ideas that go to make up the professional ideology of social work. These shared assumptions and principles are not easy to describe. Social work seems to be forever trying to capture just what it is it wishes to present as its identity to the outside world—particularly to other, often competing, professions. Casework, groupwork, community work, are seen as three methods of intervention but what is the common foundation of all these which is called social work? The

76

process of becoming a social worker which is observed in this study involved a continual groping for this common element which could never quite be captured. The students assumed that they were learning to represent a body of knowledge of some kind to the teachers in the schools but never knew quite what it was. Many of the discussions about how their intervention in the schools was proceeding were punctuated by a return to the basic question—but what exactly are we trying to say/do/achieve. The endless questions were answered, when they weren't ignored, by the inter- jection of any one of a number of what we describe as social work maxims: snatches of ideas which, together, seem to make up much of social work knowledge. Thus from our reports of meetings we read: 'Ben asked again what they were aiming to do. The super- visor replied: 'We're all liberal and progressive and we're agreed on what should be".' Some student criticism of casework followed. It appeared to them to be a 'special something' they were now sup- posed to have as a result of having heard lectures about it. The supervisor replied to this: 'Creating a relationship is the essence of social work. The greatest thing a social worker can offer is himself—nothing else matters.'

This type of idea is very helpful to students who later find them- selves in work situations where they are unable to help their clients by providing money, homes or other material needs because of the shortage of funds. To believe that the most important thing one has to offer as a social worker is oneself makes it likely that social workers will not concern themselves as much as they otherwise might with the policies and priorities of their employing authorities.

The continued search for the essence of social work probably characterised this group of students more than most students on social work courses. In most student field-placements the necessity to fulfil officially defined duties and to present formally required reports determines the nature of the job. The professional maxims of social work are then deployed around these duties to create the impression that they are 'professional' activity. The only established statutory role for social workers in schools, however, that of the education welfare officer, was denied to our students. A fear of treading on the toes of the education welfare service, inculcated by the supervisor, warned students away from adopting this role. Faced with this lack of clearly defined role, the students had only these professional maxims to resort to, and by themselves they proved an unhelpful guide to action.

In the students' estimation the high point of the project was the conference arranged at the end and entitled 'Should teachers be social workers?' Staff of the schools involved, various local officials and social workers were invited, and rather reluctantly, a few parents and pupils. The students in this project ended up confident enough of these rather ill-formed social work concepts to confer with another profession and tell them how they ought to modify their practice in the light of what social work had to say.

Disavowal of intellectuality and theoretical thinking

All these aspects of the process of becoming a social worker were underlined by the general tendency to disavow intellectuality and theoretical thinking in favour of the appreciation of the feelings that lay behind the ideas being expressed.

This avoidance of theory, especially about society and about the relationship between the individual and society, leads students to the psychological reductionism we have described, and a reliance on social work maxims, rather than an explicit analysis of the novel social situations confronting them in their fieldwork, such as in these schools. The introspective group sessions that we have described earlier led to the replacement of intellectual interchange by discussion at a largely experiential level—feelings of shared togetherness, mutual antagonism, etc. Personalities and feelings pushed out the ideas and thoughts. If heated political debate did occur, it would somehow be miraculously ended by a statement like, 'It's good that we have expressed our feelings on this issue.' The ideas and criticisms expressed are not regarded as having importance for an analysis of the problems, nor for action proposals but only in so far as they modify or clarify the relationship between the members of the group. This means that while students were ostensibly given an instrumental task in their placements their discussions of the issues involved were interpreted as having partly an expressive and partly a personally therapeutic value. Both of these motives are revealed in the following dialogue:

> Jill: The people who evaluate you can only get as much as you are willing to give. My tutor and supervisor have such different personalities.
> Felix: Ben didn't put up defences here because the group is very caring.
> Ben: Not like the tutors.
> Supervisor: Ben is afraid of his own destructiveness.
> Ben: Well, this seems to be the consensus. I suppose it might be something like that.
> Supervisor: You were afraid if you let go you'd let go good and proper. You haven't realised that the others have enough defences to stand up to you.
> Ben: It's true I've been afraid to criticise Jill. I remember once

when Felix questioned me on some of my practical work, it really hurt me. I bluffed it at the time but I admit his criticism hurt me.

Supervisor: It's no accident that it's taken us so long to get this far. We had to try each other out for a long time. Only when we feel sure enough can we be critical constructively without destroying each other. Except for Ben this would not have happened.

Because insufficient integration was achieved between the academic and practical parts of the course (and this seems commonly to be the case in social work training), the students were quick to separate the two, and take the dangerous step of regarding all forms of critical discussion as 'destructive' intellectuality. They soon learn to stereotype the intellectual and/or critical student as a trouble maker, someone who is 'cold and unconcerned'. And this becomes a further justification for the tendency already noted to use case-work principles to sort out problems between colleagues, to put a colleague who seems difficult in the place of the client. If alternative proposals are discussed thus in terms of the personality of the proposers rather than in terms of the content of the proposals, it of course reinforces the effect already noted which psychological reductionism has in the cooling out of social–structural criticism.

Making out as a social work student

We have so far attempted to describe some of the aspects of the socialisation of social work students. We have indicated the way in which they come to see themselves as professionals, with their particular theories of society and human relationships. We have indicated how these theories lead to an inappropriate way of analysing social structures and organisations, notably their place-ment schools, and the problems they faced in them.

A clash which developed between social work and teaching maxims provides an example. It was in the field of the children's behaviour that the ideas of social workers and those of the teachers most often clashed. This can be seen, for example in this quotation from the practical work supervisor: 'We as social workers are seen as the great apologists for kids' misbehaviour because we explain it in terms of family psychopathology whereas they [the teachers] just say "that kid's a bastard".' Asked about the differences the students thought that there might be between the ideas of social workers and teachers a student proffered: 'Teachers are more puni-tive—social workers have a working-through.'

The idea that social workers have in some way a different point of view on children's problems from that of teachers was an unproblematic-sounding assumption which turned out to be a major source of confusion. At no time in the project was there any real grasp of the fact that the differing ideas of the teachers and social workers about how to deal with children were closely linked to the different social situations of the teachers and social workers and to the different ways in which the children ('clients', 'pupils') were defined by them. There was no realisation that any attempt to change the definition of the problem (pupils to clients) implies at the same time that a person (teacher) previously acting upon one definition (pupil) will feel his position to be challenged, his expertise and authority to be invalidated and possibly even his reputation with his supervisors and therefore his job security to be jeopardised.

The students thus did not anticipate the resistance of teachers to their view of children's problems. They seemed to feel at first (possibly because this was the interpretation backed up by the supervisor) that there must be something they could do to increase the teachers' 'trust' in them. The supervisor told the students that if they found they had fewer problems in disciplining the pupils than the teachers, this was not because as social workers they were 'clever', but because they did not have to bear the burden of the teachers' 'institutional role'. This sort of thing could be taken as a critique of the structure which casts teachers in a role which gives them so many problems, but in fact the supervisor uses it as yet another justification for the teachers' methods, a cue to the students as to how they should interpret the happenings in the school so as to avoid making inappropriate criticisms and perhaps destroying the teachers' 'trust' in them. The supervisor argues: 'There really is a difference. You have to deal with it differently. You can't deal nicely with a miscreant in a large class because then all the others would say "Oh good!" and start to misbehave as well.' Ben objects that in the case of caning he really does think his way is right and theirs is wrong, but another student replies: 'Caning is like having to make the best use of available resources. They don't have enough counsellors, teachers and so on to deal with problems the way we do.' Here is a strange inversion of social work ideas: i.e. having to make the best use of scarce resources often causes hardship, therefore something which causes hardship (in this case, caning) is an instance of having to make the best use of scarce resources. The conversations held during meetings, the accounts members give of their situations, are full of this sort of logically invalid but convincing-sounding (in their context) inversions of general, taken-for-granted recipes. This is one of the ways the students discovered of reformulating their original interpretations of the problems they faced in order to make these interpretations acceptable simultaneously to their supervisor and to others in strategic positions, in this case the teachers. This is what is meant by 'making out'.

The students faced with this clash between the teachers' ideas and social work maxims were groping in the dark because they did not realise the extent to which theories and ideas about how an organisation can achieve its purposes are linked to the forms of organisation and authority. This means that to challenge the theories held by teachers about, for example, pupil misbehaviour, is to challenge the organisation and authority structure of the school as a whole. Instead they adopted the course of making out to any given audience (teachers, social work supervisor, fellow students) by saying what they thought the audience wanted to hear —though the process was of course not a conscious and deliberate one. Behind it is the emphasis placed in their social work training on the overriding importance of personal relationships—such as those of 'trust' between teachers and social workers—and the necessity therefore of using strategies which protect it. Another way of putting it would be to say they were in a very real sense placing the teachers themselves in a client role, i.e. seeking to casework them as their tutors and supervisors had caseworked them.

The members of the group thus came to be able to use their repertoire of social work maxims to reinterpret activities by a school that might otherwise have seemed reprehensible, and to reconcile with one another otherwise inconsistent 'making-out' acts on their part. Even when they were unable to avoid feelings of doubt, confusion and scepticism, they literally did not have available the conceptual equipment necessary to perceive the situation in any other way. They thus had to choose either to accept a view that seemed to rule out the possibility of their taking action or even understanding how the school manufactures children's problems, or to strike out blindly by expressing their feelings of discontent in unprofessional language, which, due to its colloquial, emotive nature is more susceptible to interpretation as 'anger', 'irrational response', 'immaturity', and accordingly of being attributed to the student's personality rather than to characteristics of the situation.

Thus the recipe of maxims is substituted for the alternative of a theory explaining the various contradictions the students observed in the school situation. The college provided little theoretical input into the unit of any type, least of all of a sociological nature. The schools project was not related to the students' previous lectures on formal organisations for example. Also, as their final qualification was given almost purely on social work criteria, students had little incentive to develop their ideas about social and organisational structure.

Paradoxically, as we have seen the recipe of maxims does however include *system variables*, incorporating elements of a possible radical criticism. Thus the supervisor does refer to 'resources', 'class size' and other *system variables*. As we suggested earlier she uses the 'system', factors beyond the teacher's control, however, as a whipping boy only when it is expedient to do so in order to cool the students out of their criticism of the teachers. The supervisor was able to do this because, at the college, what theoretical side there was to the students' work had exposed them both to ideas of casework and to a very limited amount of 'radical' sociological criticism of casework. The necessity for students to negotiate their identities as between college tutors espousing one or other of these opposed views had taught them how to use both sets of ideas in a purely strategic manner—a further aspect of the making-out process, if a minor one, and one in which the bargaining power of sociology is small.

The students more generally had to learn to negotiate their identities as between the college, the settlement and the schools, all of which they saw as making different demands upon them. The college was seen by the students as demanding 'high academic standards' and largely as a hostile factor. The settlement was seen to demand emotional adherence to 'social work principles', 'good professional practice', 'the nebulous aim of service' and 'involvement, commitment'. The schools' demands became clear to them more slowly, and in fact never attained a 'final' interpretation. Which of these identities did the students feel they 'really' carried? To a large extent it may be said that they didn't know. The social work 'service' identity pure and simple would not have allowed them to negotiate wholeheartedly with the schools. When they assented to the teachers' maxims (truancy today is on the rise because there's not enough discipline', 'the education welfare have so much of this welfare work to do now, they don't have time to deal with truancy') which were problematic from the point of view of social work, was this just a strategy for saving the faces of those concerned and improving relationships with the teachers, or did it represent a real change in the ideas of students? The fact that all but one of them quickly discarded what they saw to be the 'academic' identity, which favoured 'reading' and 'criticism' over 'speaking from the heart', 'taking care not to be destructive of others', meant that any analytical assessment of the structure of power and relationships in a school was impossible. So they became unsure of how they 'really felt'.

The distinction must therefore be drawn between learning *about* schools and their problems, and learning to *operate as* social work students within a school. The latter is a making-out process involving the need to take on disparate identities appropriate to the different audiences concerned, in the course of which the student may intermittently accept the reality of the maxims and myths of teaching rather than examining how these are used to maintain the structure of the educational world. In other words he 'really' agrees with the teachers some of the time, 'really' sees the head's point of view some of the time and so on. Since neither parents nor children have any power over the placement, they do not constitute an effective audience for the student. The idea of making out is essentially linked to power relationships; the maker-out must be an object to his audiences, they must be able to act upon him. Therefore the shape taken by an actor's negotiations is determined only by those audiences who can affect *him*, not by audiences he or others who designate his role *say* he should play to. But the students, for reasons we have indicated, never became aware of this and were constantly puzzled as they witnessed their own powerlessness to do anything for children and parents, no matter how well accepted they seemed to be by the school.

The politics of the placement

A comment by the unit supervisor depicts well one of her prime concerns throughout the placement and begins to offer an explanation of what happened : 'If it hasn't disturbed the fabric too much, that's good.' Schools, as we have already seen, are extremely sensitive to criticism. Research has also shown that schools play a central part in maintaining the class structure of society and that there is a wide gap between the stated aims of the school and the ways in which its organisational processes actually affect the lives of its pupils. There is a growing tendency away from the idea that it is 'home background' that makes children a problem at school towards the view that, for most children, school creates more problems than it solves.

It would not have been surprising that six often initially enthusiastic students thrown into four schools in a deprived neighbourhood, had stirred up one or two hornets nests. They might have been expected to find themselves defending the children against the head, the community against the school, or find themselves on the 'wrong' side in a number of related arguments. That these conflicts only reached the surface once, and then were hidden by the swift action of one of the heads in withdrawing from the project, is indeed remarkable. As we have suggested it was made possible by the myriad of little ways in which potentially disruptive ideas of the students were counselled out with the collaboration of the unit supervisor.

The role the unit supervisor took was to support the schools against the students consistently and methodically. 'We do want to do what they ask us in a way.' 'One must placate and grovel for the sake of relationships—everything is to be gained by not making him [the head] feel undermined.' 'In your case you don't want to talk about structures—you should put yourself at the service of the school, help them to do something better than they're already doing.' When plans were being laid for the conference of social workers and teachers at the end of the placement, students were occasionally voicing what the supervisor saw as possibly critical comments. Thus: 'I've learned about the importance of a head in a primary school.' The supervisor's comment here was 'I wouldn't like you to say that, it would be offensive to the others.' That the conference, designed to ease communication between two professions, might end up in a row between students and established headmasters was obviously to be avoided.

This illustrates two points. One, which we have already discussed, is the impediment to learning about schools caused by the necessity to negotiate with them. The other is the way in which the supervisor based in the settlement encourages the group to 'learn' in a way which helps her to present a front to the various superiors with whom she must negotiate. She is caught between the expectation of the college that she teaches and the expectation of various persons in authority in the area, that the project does not upset or be seriously critical of established practices. The supervisor teaches the students to make out because she must also make out— by teaching within certain prescribed limits. She encourages them to concentrate on thinking methodically: to 'pull your information together', 'systematize your experiences', 'locate the general points' at her meetings with them immediately preceding her own meetings with advisory committees, heads, and local authority figures to whom she wishes to present an acceptable front.

What the students are being 'taught' is determined by what will constitute a legitimately demonstrable piece of learning in the eyes of the effective audiences to the unit and by the need to placate 'important' figures in the local hierarchy. The stated aim of 'learning' is defeated by the *realpolitik* of the situation, which is that the physical possibility of the placement is partly controlled by the headmasters. We are not implying that this course is in any way unique in this: it is generally true that finding and keeping practical work placements is a major logistical problem for colleges. It may be that many social work courses are faced by dilemmas arising from the politics of the placement, and are thus limiting what students can be encouraged to learn. It seems that the emotion generated by the precariousness of the settlement's own post-Seebohm position, with the threat of its functions being taken over by new decentralised social service departments, is at least one of the reasons for the importance attributed to 'not treading on anyone's toes', 'observing hierarchies and sensitivities', and that this has helped to raise barriers to learning. It also explains the importance of 'loyalty' to the settlement. The students, once they had effectively identified with the settlement, as the supervisor encouraged them to do, were recruited into this struggle, which made it even less likely that they could ever stand back and look at the situation from any other perspective. It may also be surmised that the constant emphasis on 'relationship', 'nebulous aims of service', etc. may be explained by the ideology of the settlement as a whole and the type of work they do and by the fact that to some extent the settlement's survival depends on the polite cultivation of the goodwill of the rich and influential.

The supervisor is, therefore, not teaching—she is making out. She is indirectly telling the students what opinions will be acceptable to effective audiences, while implying that these opinions are the 'right' ones on other criteria agreed upon by herself and the students. In more serious interaction with the students she uses a form of speech which looks like a hypothesis or a generalisation, tacitly justified by her 'experience' and 'expertise', such as 'Nothing is to be gained by undermining the heads', 'the most important thing the social worker has to offer is himself, nothing else matters'; in order to instil in the students a socially acceptable response. The language-style of teaching is used to socialise, to instil ways of behaving, of making out, rather than to convey ideas and information. In this way much of the latent political and controversial content of the work is filtered out. Coupled with the establishment of the teachers in a quasi-client role, this strategy effectively shuts off from the students any possibility of the appreciation of school structure, the school's location in the power complex of local authority and social services, the ways in which children's problems are produced by the allocation of resources, and thus by power-relationships. This leads both to ineffectiveness and to confusion on the part of the students.

Because of the great influence of the particular supervisor of the project the question may be raised as to whether her views are unique and as to whether our research can have general validity as a comment on social work education in general if they are. The influence of the supervisor is clear; what is at issue is from what are her views derived, under what constraints is she operating, what interests has she to maintain in running an experimental student unit in a long-established settlement. We believe this is not a unique situation. It is a feature of social work ideology as we described it in more detail in an earlier section, that it fits in with the demands of this and similar social situations. The avoidance of the analysis of structures, the emphasis on individuals, all make it an admirable set of ideas for somebody not wishing to disturb the *status quo* or antagonise powerful interests which are important for one's own survival.

6

Ends and means
D. A. Fowler

The question, 'What is social work?' dominates the social work scene at the moment. More specifically, Ann Hartman, in a recent article, posed the question, 'What is social casework?' She concluded: 'the answer would seem to depend on whom one asks'.[1] If, indeed, this is the answer to this question, then what are social worker educators to teach about social work methods? Methods can only make sense in the context of objectives and I want to suggest, in this paper, that: (a) they are much more explicit than many social worker writers would have us believe; (b) they incorporate both a care and control objective and (c) that this latter aim, for which social workers have been unnecessarily apologetic, is both proper and defensible. Social workers, in their practice, move between the care and control position, using their judgment about the situation confronting them. To survive in the jungle of competing and conflicting values, which is the reality of life, social workers must be pragmatic. Social work has, consequently, become a happy hunting ground for the critic, often, it should be acknowledged, with good cause. Nevertheless, the way in which the nature of social work activity has been grossly oversimplified to fit theoretical assumptions about the nature of society and ideological positions must fall hard on practitioners who spend their working lives under intolerable pressure of heavy workloads, inadequate resources and poor rewards, while dealing with some of the most difficult people in society. This distorted view of social work practice is reflected in a recent article by Middleman and Goldberg,[2] where one finds social work practice thus:[3]

Social workers spend their time teaching the poor how to budget and encouraging the powerless to accept their lot in life. Their image is that of the lady who knows better than you do what is best for you and your family and has the power of the establishment to enforce her better judgement.

It is little wonder that the authors find the new recruits to social work training in America out of sympathy with this view of practice. These new recruits tended to loathe a 'profession that trusts process and perpetuates an inadequate *status quo*'.[4] They, the students, 'want to change the existing social arrangements, and they want to change them now'.[5]

The problem may be more acute in America than in Britain. However, anyone connected with student training in this country will be familiar with the issues involved—Am I to become an agent of social control or of social change? Yet social work has inhabited an uncertain world, and always will. Its operational base is at the boundary of our knowledge of human behaviour. Its ethics are ambiguous and conceptions of its role and function fluctuate according to the demands made upon it by various groups and by the vicissitudes of the society within which it operates. Social work is, in fact, caught in the classic double-bind: 'Social workers have been subject to the just and unjust criticism expressed by the public that maintains the conservative structure [of social welfare]; by the client who feels he is not served by it and by the reformer and social scientist who wants it changed.'[6]

Given a long-standing debate about the nature of social work, the current schisms differ from those of the past in a vital way. The contemporary conflict is about the ends of social work and not, as so often before, about the means. There are those who see social work as a tool for effecting radical change in the structure of our society, with social workers committed to the 'redistribution [of power] in favour of the have-nots'.[7] For these, contemporary social work practice is seen as helping clients to adjust to intolerable social conditions, imposing an alien middle-class culture upon the working-class clients (who comprise the majority of social work clientele), and maintaining an élite system. On the other hand, there are those who eschew such revolutionary aims and who insist that social work is about the individual and his adjustment to his situation within society. This quite basic predicament is one with which each of us has, in some way, to come to terms. Most of us locate ourselves, temporarily, at some point between these two extreme positions. Our location will be the outcome of our own attempts to reconcile the conflicting demands which are upon each of us. However uncertain they may be, administrators have to administer, teachers have to teach, and the practitioner has to respond to the demands of the client.

The aims of 'care' and 'control' are the institutionalised expressions of love and concern, on the one hand, and of fear and distrust of nonconformity on the other. Their joint incorporation in social work institutions and practice will ensure the permanence of a conflict for the social worker in his work with clients, between the free choice of the individual and the demands of society. The practitioner can only be pragmatic in trying to reconcile them—maintaining the integrity of the individual on the one hand, and effecting change in the person on the other. The practitioner who has to 'do' may find comfort for his pragmatism in the suggestion of Saul Alinsky that concern for the ethics of a particular action is for the indulgence of those who do not have to make the decision.[8]

Social work institutions reflect the ambivalence of society to the issue of, 'Who needs help?' or, perhaps more accurately, 'Who deserves help?' Social work theorists have acknowledged one side of the ambivalence, namely that social work activity which is the expression of care. They have tended to neglect, and even ignore, that other side which is the expression of society's concern about non-conformity. These two strands are nevertheless, evident in the emergence of social work institutions. A characteristic of most cultures is the recognition of some measure of responsibility for those in need. The definition of need varies with the value-orientation of the particular culture, but one may, nevertheless, detect an awareness of an obligation to those whose needs have been identified and accepted. As a result, societies have organised institutions for themselves which express this sense of obligation. The family, as a unit, has built into it notions of reciprocal obligations between its members. In other societies such obligations are implicit in kinship groups. Other institutions, such as religious organisations, work and interest groups, acknowledge mutual obligations in varying degrees. Yet one may still ask the question: 'Is "need" defined in terms of the individual, or in terms of the group?' 'Is our sense of obligation aroused because the person is deemed to be in need of help; because he is unable to cope, perhaps because of handicap, poverty, lack of parents etc.; or is it, in some way, related to the inability of the individual to play his full part in society, which includes meeting his obligations to others?' In other words, 'Is our helping activity designed to minister to the solidarity and welfare of the groups, of which the individual is a member, rather than to the latter's own needs?' The helping activity of social work is, therefore, best seen as a continuum having, at one end, help mobilised out of a sense of caring and recognition of responsibility to the individual in need, and, at the other end, help which is mobilised because of the perceived threat to the established order, characterised by the criminal, mentally ill, unemployed, etc. Charlotte Towle describes social work as being 'concerned with social ills. It serves groups that need to be protected, and at times, actively defended. It serves society which also seeks protection through social work.'[9] Even less attention has been devoted to its implication for social work methods.

This ambiguity in the nature of social work is reflected in the contradictory attitudes that social workers find, both among the influential members of the public and among ordinary citizens. It is a reality, together with its frustrations, with which one has to learn to live. Attempts to introduce community care programmes have been sorely hampered by the indifference and even outright opposition of the powerful, who see independent behaviour in deprived areas as something of a threat. Yet these same people have created social work organisations to achieve social purposes, have sanctioned the work of social workers and provided resources to meet these objectives. Such is the organisational context in which social workers must operate (the term social work should preclude private practice), whether it be in a voluntary or statutory agency.

This means that, in a democratic system, the aims of the social work agency will reflect the political ideology sanctioned by the electorate via the ballot box, or, in the case of voluntary organisations, by the success of the appeal for support. This oversimplifies a far more complex process in which real power is shared with various groups who participate in the work of the agency. They include social work professionals, administrators and the lay committee which controls the purse-strings. This process of policy formulation has all the ingredients for conflict between these different groups—a situation which hardly makes for unity of aims. Also, the activity, which they legitimate, is the right of the social worker to intervene in people's lives. Intervention may be at the request of a client who acknowledges the expertise of the social worker as appropriate to the resolution of his particular problem of interpersonal relationships or of his relationships with other social institutions. But it may also be—and this is particularly related to the subject of this paper—at the instance of others, such as, for example, in the case of probation. Such situations occur, of course, where the client is seen as rejecting some generally accepted norm of behaviour. Here the aim of control is predominant; a purpose which the client is hardly likely to share with the agency. What is at issue here is nothing less than the extent of the social consensus about social norms of behaviour, i.e. about acceptable and unacceptable ways of behaving in relation to others.

There are norms, basic to all societies, which enable individuals to relate to each other. Eliot Studt suggests that these relate to the 'security of the person, property and sexual behaviour'.[10] Thus, there are notions about normal and abnormal behaviour which are enshrined in mental health legislation; there are accepted norms about protection of property embodied in law and there are views held by the community about the ways in which parents should behave in relation to their children. These norms are reflected in social work objectives. They represent certain standards that are held, for example, about bringing up children and the conduct of relationships. Social work is normative and social workers, like other helping professionals such as teachers and psychiatrists, are thus socialising agents, engaged in a task which distinguishes them from, for example, scientists, with their claim to a value-free objectivity. Social work, in fact, ceases to be such, when it fails to reflect the norms of the society it serves.

The organisational context of social work carries with it accountability and responsibility exercised on behalf of the community. This has posed problems for those workers who reject organisational constraints and who would prefer to ignore, as far as possible, the presence of the agency. Nevertheless, a reality which social workers must accept is that they are employees and not free-lance, fee-charging professionals. The agency represents the extent to which society is, at that moment, prepared to extend its helping activities, and, while the worker may determine the means of achieving objectives, he has to accept that the goals themselves are determined in another place. Social work, itself, cannot, therefore, be said to be able to determine its own goal; nor is it even likely to do so in the future.

The idea of social workers being agents of social control, with responsibilities for preserving certain values, is likely to find little favour with either the activist, concerned with effecting social change for obvious reasons, or with those who model their approach on more clinical lines derived from psychotherapy, and who thus believe (fallaciously) that what they are doing is normatively neutral. Nevertheless, much recent social legislation is based upon the belief in the essential worthiness of the family and of the community, presumably because it is felt that they play a critical part in the essentially preservationist, socialisation process. Thus, the legislation concerning children locates the problem of delinquency within a family and community context. The same may be said of the legislation related to mental health. The legislation connected with domestic proceedings between husband and wife, while acknowledging the concept of irretrievable breakdown in marriage, provides the opportunity for social work intervention in pursuit of reconciliation. The whole concept of preventive services, so popular with social workers, and embodied in so many current social policies, is redolent of controls. The development of community care programmes in all fields of social work and the emergence of the Seebohm Report establishes a clear, ideological base of this kind for social work.

In a society which is becoming more complex and more fragmented with attendant social problems, those who are responsible for determining policy will continue to be concerned with the need to maintain stability and control. Social work in Britain can be said to have made use of this anxiety over recent years. For example, a major concern of society, since the end of the Second World War, has been the massive increase in juvenile delinquency. Most government inquiries (including the Seebohm Committee) have included the problem in their terms of reference. This has enabled more resources to be wrung from the government and more power to be vested in social workers on behalf of society. It is irresponsible of social work to claim that it has the prescription for solving such social problems. Society's anxiety and concern about them has made it vulnerable to influence from those who offer panaceas. A social work service, which exploits this basic insecurity within society, is likely to inherit the good will and resources of those who feel themselves so threatened, but at some cost to its independence.

So far, I have attempted to demonstrate that social control is as important an ingredient in social work as concern for the individual. It is woven into the fabric of social work organisations and has been made more explicit by recent legislation. It is a reality that the pragmatic social worker has to accept. This means that it (or the social system demanding conformity) needs to be acknowledged and made explicit, so that, as an objective, it can be challenged and discussed. Nicholas Haines sees social workers as transmitters of conventional values and suggests that social workers should make clear what these values are and 'invite criticism and discussion'.[11] Social work is so permeated by value judgments that to pretend any other is to deny that very reality which we, ourselves, always require our clients to face. By such denials the 'profession' loses credibility and becomes vulnerable to attack, not only from the social activist but also from the man in the street, because, in the absence of reality about objectives, the methods evolved will be contradictory and ineffective.

Social work educators need to share this pragmatism of the practitioner. As a social work teacher, I have to arrive at some compromise between the idealism of the student, my knowledge about the reality of practice and my own view as to the future development of social work. The situation is complicated by the accelerating pace of change in social work at present. The reorganisation of the social services and social work training after Seebohm, together with the extension of social work activity into fields of prevention, community and residential care, give rise to major issues in terms of social work methods. The explosion of information in the social sciences also offers the practitioner new frames of reference within which to view the situations confronting him. These frames of reference encompass a youth culture which is deeply concerned about the quality of life and frustrated by the nature of such issues as power, poverty and inequality. They are allied to the emergence of some articulate client groups, able to comment on the quality of services, and supported by social administrators increasingly concerned with the effectiveness of social work intervention. Such is the uncertainty and confusion which confronts social work education today.

A consequence of this current debate is that social work is in danger of becoming (as Hartman suggested in a passage cited earlier) all things to all people, and taking upon itself a responsibility not only for individuals, but also for the quality of the society in which we live. Its canvas has become vast and has far exceeded the traditional boundaries of the profession. It is little wonder, then, that students, as well as practitioners, are confused as to the nature of their professional activity and their capacity to cope with the work situation. To foster the notion that almost any activity of a socially ameliorative character can be embraced by social work is a myth, and a dangerous one at that. It suggests that social workers are entirely free to negotiate the service they provide to the client. But this is clearly not so. It is important that students, as well as practitioners, grasp the fact that 'social workers operate within the context of a particular social structure the elements of which are embodied in the agency which employs them'.[12]

Responsibility for confusion about objectives must rest, in part at least, with social work theorists. Agencies have also been guilty of not formulating their objectives more clearly. An idea of the problem for students, trying to hack their way through the semantic jungle of some social work texts, can be gained from the following attempts at a definition:

Social work is directed towards the realisation of the basic belief in the ethical and spiritual equality, freedom of individual development, freedom of choice of opportunities, fair competition, a degree of personal independence, freedom of speech, freedom of expression and communication, etc., etc.[13]

The underlying purpose of all social work efforts is to realise human power in individuals for personal fulfilment and social good and to release social power for the creation of the kind of security, social institutions and social policy which makes self-realisation possible for all men.[14]

The primary purpose of social work practice is to individualise people in the mass urban society.[15]

Such statements are so sweeping in their claims that they can hardly be regarded as statements about objectives, from which one might go on to talk about methods of work. But what is more important, they also imply in traditional fashion that social work is primarily concerned with individual care and totally ignores the issue of control. Hence the uncritical acceptance of the client-centred approach of Carl Rogers as a model, suggesting as it did that 'Therapy and authority cannot be co-existent in the same relationship'[16] and the relative neglect of the issue of authority in social work.[17] Yet another consequence was that practitioners attempted to apply methods of work in situations for which they were not intended. Perlman confronts this issue in relation to the casework method. She describes casework as:[18]

a clinical model. It is focussed on clear and present malfunctioning in single units of person and family. Its purpose is to give help when such an individual most experiences and feels present problems. Its actions are founded in conceptions of motivating powers within individuals and of how these powers are enhanced by relationships and notions, of releasing and reorganising values of identification, of talk, of emotional expression followed by reflective consideration and so on. As a clinical model it has a validity. For certain persons with certain problems, the one-to-one model cannot readily be disposed of. When casework moves into dealing with other sorts of problems e.g. crisis, socially antagonistic persons etc. and adopts new goals [prevention] its clinical model may need radical change.

Social work is a far from passive activity. It involves the social worker in decisions about the nature and degree of intervention, the tool of which is his use of a relationship between himself and the client. This process has been described, perhaps in typically ambiguous terms, by Biestek: 'the role of the caseworker is to help the client proceed from a situation which is undesirable and unacceptable to a situation which is desirable and acceptable.'[19] The ambiguity centres on the question of, 'Who defines the situation as "desirable" and "acceptable"?' Otto Pollak provides one answer, in suggesting that 'The helping process must assume a certain quality of acculturation in which the worker tries to help the client to move, at least somewhat, in the direction of the norms[20] represented by the agency.

Social workers have found difficulty in coming to terms with the authority which both society and clients invest in them. This difficulty originated partly in the particular interpretation of psychoanalytic concepts, as used in social work practice and in social work education. This negative attitude to issues of authority and influence made it difficult for social workers to be explicit about and to formulate methods of work which were directed more towards positive forms of 'people-changing' than against non-directive, insight-giving approaches. The current pursuit by social workers of a wider range of skills (in group and community work for instance) arises out of the increased responsibilities, assumed by social workers, and the growing awareness, as a result of developments in the behavioural sciences, of the forces impinging on the client. The weakening of the consensus model and the emergence of the conflict model of society pose yet another dilemma for those areas of social work activity which are related to social control functions. An interesting fact has been the difficulty experienced by Applied Social Studies courses in filling probation streams from applicants who have been exposed to social science teaching. Yet those courses designed for students with no social science background, appear to have experienced no difficulties in this area. New theories about the nature of society, together with the growth in understanding of the significance of power structures and minority groups, coalesce in the student and give rise to highly critical attitudes about the contemporary social structure. As a result, methods of social work and, in particular, social case-work, are seen as some subtle form of brainwashing; while other forms of social work, particularly those associated with community work, are more favoured, in that there is an assumption that social workers in these fields are more responsive to the community needs.

Casework, groupwork, community work and residential work are united by their use of the relationship between the social worker and his client. Any process which operates through the medium of personal relationships acknowledges and utilises the inequality of influence which exists between the providers and the recipients of service. In the casework situation, one cannot dispute that individuals, interacting with each other, influence one another, and the role of the social worker is paramount. Equally, one cannot dispute the significance of the relationship of the group's leader to the group, and his use of the role to influence the activities of the group. 'Experiences in groups create the opportunity for professional intervention that utilises the process of interaction for the purposes of change in much the same way as in the casework relationship.'[21] The influence of the community worker must also be acknowledged in community work: 'If the professional worker is accepted, liked and trusted, persons identifying with him will attend meetings he feels are worthwhile, will cooperate with others because he approves of such cooperation.'[22] Ross goes on to describe the process as 'not essentially different from the rapport which the caseworkers attempts to establish with the client'.[23]

All forms of social interaction are attempts by individuals, groups or communities, to influence others. In all our attempts at inter-action we try to influence another's perception of ourselves. Influence is therefore central to any form of social life, so that social workers have no need to feel guilty about the fact that they do exert influence. However, they do need to concern themselves with the ends to which this influence is directed. These are matters about which social workers should satisfy themselves when apply-ing for jobs. The fact that they are legitimated and sanctioned by society does not absolve them from such scrutiny. For those who require further reassurance, it could perhaps be suggested that social work intervention is a more acceptable means of intervention than some of the methods that society has used in the past to deal with its nonconformists. Yet influence is something which cannot be wholly legislated for. It is something which we allow others to exert upon us. A significant person is one whose influences we accept. Social workers strive to become significant persons to their clients.

Becoming a significant person as a social worker requires a com-bination of attitudes and understanding, and skill in communicating them. Lee Thayer suggests: 'Our human competencies depend ultimately upon the adequacy with which we can be com-municated with and the adequacy with which we can communicate with others.'[24] Yet Howard Parad suggests that social workers are somewhat lacking in such abilities—'How many brief service case-closings are really unplanned terminations—cases apparently closed because the client's major concern with the precipitating stress and the worker's concern with the underlying problems do not come together in a meaningful relationship.'[25] This is hardly surprising when one considers that the field of communication theory has been largely ignored by social work.[26] This is in contrast to, for example, teaching, management, advertising and the media. It is, again, related to lack of clarity about objectives and, perhaps, to a fear of being seen as manipulators which makes us reluctant to admit that we have any clear aims. But how can social work develop an adequate theory about practice when it is so vague and ambivalent about what it wants to communicate?

If social work can surmount this first obstacle, it can then go on to equip its practitioners with the skills of communication. This would enable them to communicate more effectively with their clients whether as individuals, groups or communities. A wider range of behavioural science knowledge would then be available, not excluding that connected with behaviour modification. The term 'social work methods' would then have some meaning. But more straight thinking on objectives must come first.

Because this so rarely happens, social workers find themselves in a dilemma from which they attempt to escape by using the terms 'treatment' and 'therapy' to describe their work. The use of these terms, implying as they do a sickness model, has enabled social workers to rationalise the care/control dichotomy. The problem is located in some malfunctioning of the client's personality. Value conflicts, such as those implicit in delinquent behaviour, have been re-interpreted as individual malfunctioning or sickness in much the same way as in certain countries the definition of mental illness has been extended to include expressions of a deviant political philosophy. This is not to deny that the sickness model has some relevance to some problems, but to acknowledge the existence of other ways of understanding some situations. What the sickness model does do, however, is enable social workers to believe that they have resolved the care/control dichotomy. It enables them to see control as if it were in the client's interest, and so avoid the reality of the situation.[27]

Such terms as 'treatment' and 'therapy', used in social work situations, are frequently value judgments masquerading as 'scientific', clinical judgments. As such, they act as blinkers, limiting the frame of reference of the social worker. Basing one's approach to clients on such a model poses many problems for the client. Bernstein suggests, for example, that 'treatment' requires that the client has the capacity to verbalise his problem.[28] He suggests further that the idea of 'therapy' requires that the client should involve himself in the establishment of new relationships which are highly complex in character, requiring a capacity in the client to make sophisticated connections between events.[29] Bernstein argues that, because of class differences in the use of language and the attribution of meaning, the 'therapy' situation would cause great stress for a (working-class) client because of the high level of anxiety generated by the form of social relationship. It might even be said that the form of social relationship is felt as 'persecutory'.[30] This would seem to be particularly important in view of the predominantly working-class composition of social work workloads. The difficulty of reconciling those social work activities, especially those connected with the growing use of volunteers, which do not readily fit into the treatment/therapy model, exposes still further the limitations of this approach.

Social workers and clients come together to engage in a particular task. Consumer studies suggest that the nature of this task is difficult for clients to understand.[31] A greater degree of specificity about goals would probably lead to clarity on both sides, thereby enabling the social worker to engage in a real choice of methods of achieving the task, and enabling the client to understand the nature of the activity in which he is to become involved and what is expected of him. It is the client, after all, who has to achieve the task. Eliot Studt suggests that the 'increased use of the task concept by social workers (requiring as it does the naming of the activity) adds to the precision and power of our developing practice theory'.[32]

Such an approach requires that social work educators do not ignore the conflicts that surround the normative and controlling base of social work. We cannot allow our students to emerge from training courses ill-prepared to face and cope with the conflicts which they will meet in practice. Letters written by viewers of the BBC documentary 'The Block' give some idea of the reality, in terms of attitudes, which social workers have to face in their practice:[33]

'I am curious to know who paid the cost of the luxurious funeral of the young baby. Chief mourners, richly decorated hearse and funeral cars are not paid for by the State or by a person living below the poverty line.'

'The message I got from this programme was the less you do, the more help you get from the Welfare and Voluntary Organisations. So let's get our priorities right, let's help them who, like my parents and many others, really tried and got nothing.'

These examples may be somewhat extreme but there is ample evidence to suggest that they are not untypical. Lay attitudes have not moved very far from the concept of the 'deserving poor' and, in this respect, social work practice leads rather than reflects public opinion.

Yet social work is about conflict, its resolution or containment. Conflict, not only in the context of client groups, but also conflict about basic issues surrounding means and ends of social work. The existence of such conflicts, and the ways in which they are dealt with in a social work course, is potentially a very useful learning experience for the student. However, it requires social work teachers to be more explicit about the base from which they approach social work. Such a dialogue situation provides the opportunity for staff and students to examine the nature of such conflicts and the ways in which they can be contained or resolved.

If social work is about conflict, then the contribution of social work practice to its resolution or containment is by way of intervention and the exercise of influence. With this as a starting point, a social work methods course becomes credible in so far as we can identify as an objective the task of providing the student with the competence and skills to intervene effectively. Nevertheless possession of, and the responsibility for imparting, such skills, leave both practitioner and teacher with the moral dilemma concerning the ends to which such skills may be directed. The practitioner may, and indeed often does, use his superior knowledge and skills to encourage some measure of conformity to widely accepted norms. I have shown earlier that this is an inescapable aspect of social work practice. Others would see their function more in terms of passing on skills and knowledge to clients, in order to strengthen them in coping with social demands or competing in social conflict situations; or perhaps presenting themselves to clients as vehicles, through which the clients may more effectively influence their social environment. These alternative conceptions of social work practice are both legitimate and also share a common methodology, thus providing the practitioner with the opportunity of flexibility in his approach. Most take advantage of this, and, in spite of the fact that the present institutional structure of social work favours the former rather than the latter two approaches, tend not to adopt extreme positions but rather choose to move between them. They tend to occupy a middle ground, respecting the needs of the client and also acknowledging their responsibilities to society. A role of the social worker might thus be that of a mediator exercising his influence on all parties to the conflict. The point of intervention and the direction of his influence is the product of the practitioner's judgment. The burden of responsibility carried by the social worker is thus a heavy one, and we need to concern ourselves with the balance struck between the needs of the individual and those of society. Robin Huws Jones adds a timely note of caution: 'The social worker's job is to reconcile the needs of society and of the deviant individuals. In this he must beware especially when he is highly esteemed by the establishment.'[34] The concept of being professional, with its attendant code of ethics and service commitment, plays an important part in the decision-making activities of the practitioner. It ensures that intervention is kept within limits which are tolerable both to the client and to society.

Notes

1 Ann Hartman, 'But what is social casework?', *Social Casework*, July 1971.
2 Ruth R. Middleham and Gale Goldberg, 'The interactional way of

presenting generic social work concepts', *Journal of Education for Social Work*, vol. 8, no. 2, Spring 1972.

3 Ibid.

4 Ibid.

5 Ibid.

6 Carol H. Meyer, *Social Work Practice*, Collier-Macmillan, New York, 1973; *A Response to the Urban Crisis*, Free Press, New York, 1970.

7 John Ward, 'The Haves and Have-nots', *Observer*, 15 October 1972.

8 S. Alinsky, *Rules for Radicals*, Random House, New York, 1972.

9 Charlotte Towle, *The Learner in Education for the Professions*, University of Chicago Press, 1954.

10 Eliot Studt, 'Education for Social Workers in the Correctional Field', vol. 5, Curriculum Study Project Report, Council on Social Work Education, New York, 1959.

11 Nicholas Haines, *Freedom and Community*, Macmillan, London, 1966.

12 Olive Stevenson, 'Knowledge', paper given to Study Course of Social Work Teachers Sponsored by the CCTC at Bournemouth, March 1971.

13 W. A. Friedlander, *Concepts and Methods of Social Work*, Prentice-Hall, Englewood Cliffs, 1958.

14 Ruth Smalley, *Theory for Social Work Practice*, Columbia University Press, 1967.

15 C. Mayer, *Social Work Practice—A Response to the Urban Crisis*, Free Press, New York, 1970.

16 C. Rogers, *Counselling and Psychotherapy*, Houghton Mifflin, Boston, 1942.

17 R. Foren and R. Bailey, *Authority in Social Casework*, Pergamon Press, Oxford, 1968.

18 Helen Perlman, 'Review of method', *Social Work* (US), vol. 10, 1965.

19 F. P. Biestek, *The Casework Relationship*, Allen & Unwin, London, 1963.

20 Otto Pollak, 'A Family Diagnosis Model' (1960), in E. Younghusband (ed.), *Social Work with Families*, Allen & Unwin, London, 1965.

21 Carl M. Shafer in 'General Systems Approach: Contributions towards an Holistic Conception of Social Work', in Gordon Hearn (ed.), *Teaching Social Work Practice in an integrated Course*, Council on Social Work Education, New York, 1969.

22 Murray G. Ross, *Community Organization, Theory Principles and Practice*, second edition, Harper & Row, New York, 1967.

23 Ibid.

24 Lee Thayer, *Communication and Communication Systems in Organisations, Management and Interpersonal Relations*, Richard D. Insin Inc., Homewood, Illinois, 1968.

25 Howard J. Parad, 'Preventive Casework: Problems and Implications in Crisis Intervention', in H. J. Parad (ed.), *Selected Readings*, Family Service Association of America, New York, 1965.

26 Peter R. Day, *Communication in Social Work*, Pergamon Press, Oxford, 1972.

27 Howard Jones, 'The Informed Conscience: in Search of Social Welfare', Inaugural Lecture, University College, Cardiff 1973.

28 Basil Bernstein, *Class, Codes and Control, Vol. 1, Theoretical Studies towards a Sociology of Language*, Routledge & Kegan Paul, London, 1971.

29 Ibid.

30 Ibid.

31 J. E. Mayer and N. Timms, *The Client Speaks*, Routledge & Kegan Paul, London, 1970.

32 Eliot Studt, 'Social work theory and implications for the practice of methods', *The Council on Social Work Education Reporter*, June 1968.

33 Readers' letters printed in the *Radio Times* 7-13 October 1972 in connection with the programme 'The Block' shown on BBC 1 Television on 19 September 1972.

34 Robin Huws Jones, Neely Memorial Lecture, 'Social Values in a Changing Society', given in Cleveland, Ohio, published by International Schools of Social Work, 1969.

7

Welfare rights and social work: ambivalence in action

R. G. Walton

The 1960s generated a turmoil in social work only equalled by the multifarious developments in the 1860s and 1870s. In both periods there was a new consciousness in society. Darwinism and germinating socialist philosophies were penetrating traditional ways of thinking then just as the popularisation of existentialism, the revulsion from institutionalised politics and the rebellion against bureaucratic organisations have led to attempts to evolve new social forms today. In both periods many new social organisations were attempting to influence, if not destroy, old institutions, and undertaking tasks which the existing institutional structure seemed ill-equipped to cope with. There are nevertheless significant differences and it is against the background of such differences that the 'welfare rights' approach to welfare needs to be seen.

The nineteenth century produced social welfare agencies of varying ideals and form such as the children's organisations, the Charity Organisation Society, and the settlements—the response to individual and social needs, with a religious ideal of help as a prime motivation for individuals and organisations. There was a positive outlook, with a hope for better things to come, and a whittling away of the worst aspects of the Poor Law. Many philanthropists believed that the impulse to charity, expressed in voluntary organisations, should and could deal with social problems given good administration and co-ordination. Many of the voluntary organisations expanded rapidly during the late nineteenth century and the charitable worker of the time had to know his way through the voluntary system and the Poor Law if he was to be able effectively to help those in need. Helen Bosanquet in *Rich and Poor* writes: 'one great qualification for the charitable worker is that he should know where to go for help and advice on the difficult case he comes across, and that he should be willing to accept that advice.'[1]

In the twentieth century the situation has become more complex. Superimposed on the voluntary welfare pattern we have a broad public welfare system helping large numbers of people through massive and elaborate administrative systems. In the 1960s the development of organisations helping the poor and homeless—such as CPAG, DIG, Shelter and the Claimants' Union—has taken place in this changed context. Not only has the social worker to master the complexities of an enlarged public and voluntary welfare system, but he also works in a situation in which a major part of voluntary organisation effort is centred on a critique of (mainly state) welfare organisations in terms of their ideology, function in society, administrative practice, and deficiencies in the extent and distribution of benefits. Until the 1930s voluntary organisations had very mixed feelings about the growth of the public sector of welfare, a growth very actively opposed by the COS in earlier days.[2] Now the welfare state exists and debate has shifted, from being about whether it should exist, to discussing what kind of welfare state we should strive for in terms of quantity and quality, and its meaning for its beneficiaries, potential as well as actual.[3]

The scale and complexity of the modern welfare system contrasts strongly with that of the nineteenth century, but it would be false not to pick out continuities in tradition. Helen Bosanquet, as many social workers do today, saw an important function of the social worker in being knowledgeable about, and able to use, the many sources of help available to individuals and families. Also, many of the nineteenth-century charitable workers and organisations were critical of the major public welfare institution—the Poor Law—and campaigned vigorously for its improvement. However, a fundamental difference in the period after the Second World War was the employment of the majority of social workers by statutory authorities rather than voluntary organisations, which has affected their attitudes towards becoming involved closely in a critique of the public welfare system. It is for this reason that those social workers critical of society and the present social services have tended to channel their energy into professional association activities. Alternatively, they have formed groups like Case Con whose contributors combine marxist analysis with a traditional trade-union attitude to the way in which social workers bargain over salaries and service conditions. The large cities, especially London, have been the scene of the most open conflict between social workers and their employers because of the way in which broad social problems produce the daily load of individual misery that social workers are coping with.[4]

This is the setting in which a discussion of welfare rights must take place, and the questions I shall be trying to answer concern the nature of the welfare rights approach, whether this development is of a strategic or tactical kind, and the involvement of social workers with this approach to welfare.

The meaning of 'welfare rights' needs to be clarified before embarking on other issues, as welfare rights are talked about in many senses. The concept implies that welfare rights are a special category of social rights. If we examine the welfare component in the concept first, there is the assumption that an organised system of benefits and services exists which contributes in some way (financial, health, housing) to the welfare of different user groups. A problem of any definition of welfare is that of defining standards of service (quantity and quality). Once minimum standards (in an absolute survival sense) are attained for all, how are relative standards set? Whose norms prevail? An additional problem is that of the impossibility of actually measuring the welfare and satisfaction of any individual or of adding or subtracting one individual's welfare to the welfare of another. We have to adopt the imperfect device of taking external attributes of any individual's life or social survey responses as indicators of a person's welfare.[5] To the British empirical tradition it is acceptable thus to by-pass this problem, especially now when neo-utilitarianism is such a strong force in economics, welfare and political life. Cost-benefit analysis and many other budgetary approaches often depend on crude utilitarian principles, but it is at our peril that we forget the subtler philosophical problems involved.

Any social welfare system assumes that individuals have rights: citizens are entitled to benefit from community services to maintain a given standard of life. These rights are of two kinds. There are, first, the category of natural rights, as laid down for instance in the UN Declaration of Human Rights or the United States constitution, which can be derived from a humanistic or religious ethic. They are expressed in absolute or ideal terms, and grounded in a conception of what it is to be a human being, and the social conditions which permit the highest fulfilment of human potential and creativity. Social justice is built into concepts of human rights by insisting that all individuals should share equitably in the community's resources as a means of realising individual potential in a constructive social order.[6] There is, second, a category of rights which are the legal entitlements to education, financial help, health services, and social work help which are embodied in laws, and in the regulations, practical rules and conventions of welfare agencies.[7] There is always a dynamic tension between natural and legal rights and ultimately legal rights are dependent upon, and established by appeal to, natural rights.

We can take this a stage further by asserting that, since natural rights are always expressed by the law in a particular historical context, this expression will always be imperfect. We may have an absolute conception of what man ought to have and be, but his legal rights are always limited in practice by finite physical and social resources, by selfishness and the unequal distribution of power. Thus welfare forms will always be transitional because the problems, application of analysis and reinterpretation of natural rights, and the socio-technical possibilities will be continually in flux. Welfare institutions are a consequence of the sense of individual and community obligation and benevolence towards others, and are always limited by the degree of benevolence in the community and by social and economic resources. Eugen Pusic in a wide-ranging discussion of the fusion of welfare and rights analyses the gradual merging of thinking about human rights and the welfare field : [8]

> While human rights were far-reaching in their abstract
> implications—though in practical life widely honoured in
> the breach—welfare measures were from the start
> practical and concrete enough although often woefully
> inadequate in scope and based on all sorts of
> antiquated ideologies. While the proponents of human
> rights were often unable to translate their correct reasoning
> into reality, the reality of progress, even if smaller scale,
> was achieved by welfare—frequently for the wrong
> reasons.

Pusic sees the bonding of human rights and welfare as incomplete and sees as a first task in the institutionalising influence of welfare, the need is to 'establish minimum standards of welfare as a human right'.

Bearing this analysis in mind leads me to distinguish short-term and long-term aspects of welfare rights. Thus a short-term welfare rights approach is concerned with maximising the use and effectiveness of established benefits, particularly financial and material, but also of other benefits (e.g. health, education).[9] The long-term approach is concerned with establishing new welfare rights and with modifying the purpose and practices of welfare institutions more fundamentally in the light of changing social and economic conditions. This assumes that a major divergence exists from principles of social justice and natural right.

We have moved from a situation in the nineteenth century when the main form of benevolence was private philanthropy and charity to our present twentieth-century state where public welfare systems are a prevailing and complex feature of modern life. Social work was established in the age of philanthropy and has had to adapt to the new situation. It used to be concerned with helping the respectable poor independent of a harsh Poor Law, and improving conditions under the Poor Law. Now social work has as one of its central functions to help the poor, deprived and distressed to use the public welfare system to the full, but seeks also to reform it.[10]

This line of thought needs one further clarification before I outline what I consider to be key components in a welfare rights approach which are of relevance to social work. Welfare rights should be a concern of all citizens, beneficiary groups, professional welfare workers and social workers. Social workers are not alone in their concern and should ally themselves with these other individuals and groups.

Social workers and their agencies are avoiding a moral obligation, at this juncture in social welfare, if they turn aside from the tasks implied by a welfare rights approach. What are its essential components? What kind of armoury can social workers draw on and what tasks are implied? The main components are:

1 The organisation of an efficient system of information and advice.

2 The adoption of roles of advocacy and mediation by individuals.

3 The adoption of 'corporate advocacy' by social work agencies.

4 Supporting the development of beneficiary pressure groups.

5 Using a community work approach at a neighbourhood level.

6 Reform of existing social provision and establishment of new welfare rights.

7 Research into the services: knowledge, availability and effectiveness of welfare benefits and services.

Information and advice

The need for an efficient system of information and advice derives from the mutliplicity of benefits and services and their complexity. The functional organisation of welfare means that citizens may be entitled to a wide range of benefits and services. In this country the problems have never been tackled systematically. Apart from the Citizens' Advice Bureaux[11] and the recent experiments with Family Advice Centres[12] most welfare agencies have seen their responsibility as limited to giving information and advice about their own services. Thus, when housing problems were seen to be acute, Housing Advisory Centres were established in many local authorities. Similarly for chronically sick and disabled people legislation in 1970 imposed a duty on the local authorities to inform potential beneficiaries of the services available. Because of inefficiencies in the supply of information, independent groups such as Child Poverty Action Group and Shelter have established information and advisory services located in stalls and advisory centres in shopping areas and neighbourhoods.

In spite of the valuable development work of CAB its geographical coverage is patchy and the same criticism applies even more to the services of the other voluntary bodies. That there is a need for radical review of the confused array of information services is recognised by many people. The problems mentioned above can be tackled only by central government directive, and by local planning and co-ordination. They will never be solved until a duty is laid on local authorities to provide general welfare information and advice services.[13] This would require only fairly brief legislation but would ensure that every local authority would have to consult all existing voluntary and statutory welfare agencies in its area and plan a co-ordinated service which guaranteed impartiality, accessibility, accuracy and comprehensiveness. The responsibility would be clearly allocated but the administrative and service pattern would necessarily depend on the needs of the particular area.

The relationship of the social worker to the advice and information system is complex. The first issue is that of the individual social worker as a professional with accurate information about benefits and services. There seems good reason to doubt whether many social workers do in fact possess this kind of knowledge in spite of the fact that the study of the social services is an integral part of social work training. Janet Streather, writing in *Social Work Today*[14] gave a case illustration in which a divorced woman had been visited by several social workers since 1967, none of whom had spotted that her weekly income fell far short of her needs as calculated against supplementary benefit levels; a letter and telephone call secured a substantial increase in her allowance. Olive Stevenson in her recent study of social work and the Supplementary Benefits scheme was also dissatisfied with the knowledge which the majority of social workers had of the scheme.[15] The implication is that during training social workers should spend more time studying benefits and gaining knowledge and experience of the administrative system. If this were achieved we might be able to guarantee that any person in contact with a social worker would at least be obtaining their entitlements to benefits and services, apart from any help offered with emotional and social relationship problems. The British Association of Social Workers played their part by running a series in *Social Work Today* in 1972/3 entitled, 'For your client's benefit'. There is no doubt that since the Fabian Pamphlets by Tony Lynes and David Bull[16] there has been a growing awareness of the necessity for social workers to be well informed about the benefits, and many training courses are making special efforts to ensure that this component is given sufficient weight.

The second issue is the fact that the vast majority of beneficiaries are not clients of social workers. Therefore, social workers have a responsibility to work for an efficient system of information and advice for the general public, which includes information about benefits and services. Whether this is modelled on a modified CAB or the Family Advice Centre is not the crucial issue. A. S. Kahn and his colleagues showed clearly in their study of information and advice services that needs and patterns of service may legitimately vary in different areas.[17] But the more inefficient the general system of information and advice is, the more social workers will be involved in rectifying the balance.[18]

To give these developments a sharp push forwards in social work agencies, a number of writers (e.g. J. Streather, D. Bull) have suggested the appointment of welfare rights officers in social services departments. Some departments have done this, but unless the focus is on supporting all the staff with a back-up system of information and expertise, there could be the danger of simply establishing a further specialism, leaving the front-line social worker not fully competent in this area of work.

Adopting roles of mediation and advocacy

The functions of mediation and advocacy are interdependent in welfare rights work, the former indicating a more impartial, independent stance as broker, communication channel, arbitrator, and the latter implying a more positive espousal of the beneficiary's view and problems, and an active pursuance of the interests of the welfare claimant.[19] Crucial to an understanding of roles of mediation and advocacy in welfare are the notions of commitment and community sanction. In the present structure of our welfare services, the roles of mediator/advocate are not fixed by community sanction. There are a wide variety of situations in which a family member, friend or representative of a trade union, a lawyer, a social worker or counsellor may find themselves negotiating with officials in welfare organisations on behalf of clients. Yet most users of social services are not associated with consumer groups, nor do they have automatic access to the services of a mediator or advocate. A major assumption of welfare rights workers is that, generally, beneficiaries have little power and influence compared with the officials in welfare bureaucracies and that mediation and advocacy are important ways of redressing this balance. The way in which mediators and advocates interpret and act in their roles depends on the strength of their commitment to this view of the beneficiary as the underdog in the system, or alternatively their commitment towards supporting analytical views of the functions of welfare systems as institutions for regulating and controlling the lower echelons of the class structure.[20]

How are the roles of mediator and advocate convergent or divergent with the other roles of social workers? B. Wootton[21] and R. Lubove[22] both discuss the traditional roles of social workers as part of the broad welfare system and see that historically social workers' knowledge of the social welfare system is a major field of expertise in its own right, to be used in the interests of clients. B. Wootton goes so far as to see the social worker as a poor man's lawyer. I would support the view that mediatory roles have been at the core of the British social work tradition and are sanctioned by social work organisations. Disagreement emerges about whether mediatory roles should extend in the direction of advocacy. Individual social workers are confused by the ambivalence of their social work agencies towards advocacy. Social work agencies are part of the welfare system and often put conventional and administrative restraints on advocacy; this, at least, is how many social workers see the situation. Social security and housing workers are their colleagues, but they nevertheless have a commitment to the client in his battles with the social security or housing system. There is a further conflict in that individual social workers are not clear whether they should extend their mediation and advocacy to individuals within their own area of work who are not clients of social work agencies. Advocacy is time-consuming and most social workers have to arrange their priorities in order to deal first and foremost with statutory and agency commitments. Another important constraint is the fear of publicity about open conflict between social work agencies and other welfare agencies, which leads individual social workers to sense the limits of mediation and advocacy in a particular agency. This fear may well arise from the desire of social services departments not to have their own shortcomings attacked by other welfare organisations.

The concept of advocacy has a legal origin. Yet we should be clear that in its use by the welfare rights movement it has not the legal connotation of a kind of 'game'. Within the legal system the role of advocate is institutionalised. The traditional advocate is not committed to the client except in so far as the immediate legal problem is concerned, and he does not necessarily believe in the rightness or wrongness of the client's cause. He is employed to put the best possible case within the established code of law. The welfare rights advocate is by contrast committed to a certain view of the welfare system and is committed to the beneficiary in a wider sense than the immediate welfare problem might suggest. It is possible to support either interpretation and relate it to a discussion of professionalism. What is clear, however, is that in social work agencies the roles of mediation and advocacy should be sanctioned and institutionalised, but without adopting a purely games-playing philosophy.[23]

The adoption of corporate advocacy

To achieve a framework in which individual social workers can be effective mediators and advocates necessitates further development of policy in the area of welfare rights. This should cover all the aspects of the welfare rights approach listed above.

Until a social work agency has clarified the acceptable limits to mediation and advocacy, the management team and individual social workers will exhibit confusion and hesitation about such activities and relegate them to peripheral, leisure-time and possibly subversive interest. The social worker needs to know that he has the sanction and support of his department in this area of work.

The agency should not only establish a welfare rights policy (which means in local authority social services departments a specialist appointment, and as proof of some commitment by the authority, the acceptance of supervisory responsibility by an Assistant Director or Principal Social Services Officer) for its own internal activities, but a policy also governing its external relations with other welfare agencies. The justification for this is that poor standards and gaps in health, education, housing, social security often become apparent in experience with social work clients. Social services departments should not simply respond by expanding to take up the slack or to paper over the cracks. There is a general responsibility for corporate advocacy to operate within the structure of the local authority in relation to its own services and those of centrally organised welfare agencies.

This pattern of thinking has implications for social work training —political understanding and action is an essential parameter for exploration, in relation to the welfare rights field generally, and more specifically the management and orientation of social work agencies in the welfare system. Also, professional social work associations have a triple responsibility in this sphere: to explore welfare rights roles in relation to the development of social work; to provide support to individual services or groups of social workers; and to encourage social work agencies to establish a policy climate and framework which sanctions and develops these activities.

The support and development of beneficiary pressure groups

Advocacy and mediation essentially interpose other individuals and groups between beneficiaries and providers, whether these be social workers, other professionals, academics, or middle-class volunteers. Recent years have seen a growing body of opinion arguing that consumer participation must be a vital element in the development of welfare services.[24] The language of consumption is an unfortunate incorporation from commercial language because it has the connotations of passive recipients of welfare and begs the question of what it is to be a consumer of welfare. We would do well to discard a terminology which sees consumers as people to whom we sell our welfare, and to bear in mind the fundamental criticisms by Titmuss of treating welfare as a consumer good in the economic sense. I will therefore talk about welfare beneficiaries rather than consumers as being both a more neutral and a more accurate description of those who have actual or potential entitlement to welfare services.[25]

The centralising tendencies of the health services, and of bureaucratic management based on very broad functional categories, militate against the involvement by beneficiaries in welfare except by being passively processed by the system. That beneficiaries are beginning to raise their voices, are beginning to develop a consciousness that their status and influence could be greater, has emerged as a reaction against these centralising forces. At present their voice is either too soft or too raucous; their frustration leads them to diffidence or excessive demands. How can we move in the direction of greater and more balanced involvement?

The first way is by providing support to beneficiary organisations and serving as a catalyst in bringing about an extension of the range of beneficiary groups.[26] Thus welfare agencies should nourish groups which institutionalise criticism and which lobby the welfare agency on behalf of the poor, the handicapped, the elderly, and the sick. Financial support is already given to many such groups, but frequently this is to extend services by voluntary help rather than encourage criticism. It seems incongruous that in the field of individual development we assume that an important sign of maturity is the willingness to adapt to criticism from others, whereas in our institutional life success is often judged by the ability to reject and deflect criticism.

Criticism and involvement is a function of access to information. Therefore a precondition for extending involvement in evaluating, planning and administering services is a greater flow of information from welfare agencies. It calls also for an involvement of beneficiaries beyond the formal committee level, giving an opportunity for a wider variety of beneficiaries to contribute to and influence the direction of welfare policies and their implementation.[27] The effect of all this would be to break down the oligarchic control of welfare, sharing that control with those for whom the service is supposed to exist. These are ways of altering the professional/beneficiary (expert/layman) relationship which would enable a more fruitful monitoring and development of welfare services within limits set by party policies and programmes. Beneficiaries would then become a major third force influencing both elected representatives and the officials. A side-effect could be a growing political awareness and active interest in traditional political processes. Problems there are, no doubt, and it will take time to discover viable forms and processes for this third force to establish itself. But until this happens the decisions of elected members and officials will remain relatively unresponsive to the ideas and feelings of beneficiaries about their problems and their views about alternative solutions. So far, local authority social services departments and probation departments have taken only the most faltering steps in this direction, generally following traditional patterns of bureaucratic administration. The planning ethos militates against this line of attack because it leaves the experts exposed and appears to diminish traditional political power. But the opportunity is there if social work agencies have the strength of commitment to seize it.

Using a community work approach at the neighbourhood level

Much of the argument above hinges upon the assumption that individuals do have welfare rights in relation to their needs and problems, and also have a further right to share in the processes which determine the quality and extent of community obligation and service towards them. Related to this is the assumption that present decision-making and administrative structures and processes frequently ignore this right and in practice tend to conceive of the beneficiary as a passive object. There is need for a countervailing influence from beneficiaries to rectify this situation and some ways of achieving this have been reviewed.

Another way of achieving greater involvement is through community work. It has always been a hallmark of social work theory that the client (whether conceived of as an individual, a group or a community) should share in the identification of problems and in the reaching of solutions. There is sufficient evidence from many studies that in most administrative areas there are pockets with a higher incidence of social problems.[28] Frequently the standard of environment, education, housing and employment opportunities in these areas is low. Thus, the problems are, in part, of a social rather than an individual character. One of the major tasks of community workers is to sensitise those in the neighbourhood to their conditions and the low standard of service they receive from the welfare agencies. The next step—often a difficult one—is to assist the community to mobilise its own resources, an activity aimed among other things at influencing public bodies to provide more adequate services. Community associations, community action groups, settlements, housing groups, tenants' associations and officially sponsored projects under the Urban Aid and Education Priority schemes have been involved in this kind of activity.[29] What has yet to emerge is any form of community action that will serve as a paradigm for use in most areas rather than a marginal form of service in a relatively small number of areas of high social need. Yet the enlargement of local government areas and the consequent decreasing control by the citizen will strengthen the growth of a wide variety of community-based organisations and actions, which at some stage will have to be institutionalised in formally organised neighbourhood or community councils. For the moment we are at the stage where patterns of control and communication between citizens and the public services are emerging and differentiating themselves, and we may be certain that some injustice will be the result in the short term. Communities and neighbourhood groups will compete in the priorities jungle, and the most active and powerful may well corner a more than equitable share of limited community resources rather than substantially enlarge the total resources available. We must not expect too much from community work even though there are potentially strong links with the welfare rights field. Local and national organisation is weak and community workers are not able to make an impact on income levels.

A key contribution can be made to welfare rights by community work if it succeeds in stimulating local government and other welfare agencies into looking at the neighbourhood as a whole, provoking interdepartmental thinking and co-operation. Community organisations and their workers can also promote the development of information and advice services, which can serve as a base for wider community action. Advice and information services can be an important stage in the process of creating social awareness of neighbourhood problems and the exploration of corporate action to deal with them, drawing on resources within the community and external to it.

Up to now one of the major difficulties underlying the involvement of community work with welfare rights is the concentration of community projects on particular service programmes such as play-groups and voluntary help schemes. In the statutory sphere, probably in social services departments, community work programmes may simply provide essential community services and act as a focus for drawing on voluntary action rather than developing a new consciousness of the potential for action within the community. Community work is seen more as a way of saving ratepayers' money: much less as a way of providing a critique of existing welfare agencies. G. Popplestone sees clearly the problems posed for community workers in acting along the lines described, and emphasises that their success may well depend on how much caseworkers are willing to support community work as a means of challenging the existing power structures. Activity in the field of welfare rights is an element in social work which could draw community workers and caseworkers together in a common aim.

Social reform

Advice and information, advocacy and mediation, the development of beneficiary pressure groups, and community work are, it must be admitted, mainly tactical elements in a welfare rights approach. They tend to concentrate on immediate problems of inequitable provision and administration within the welfare system.

Social workers, located as they are at the perimeter or interstices of broader welfare services, frequently deal with the individuals and groups whose needs the bureaucratically administered welfare system is insufficiently articulated and responsive to meet. Thus they will always have a crucial role in monitoring in a direct and practical way the effects of welfare provision in the lives of individuals. But in a battle tactical manoeuvres form an integral part of overall strategy for social reforms. However, there is a significant difference between the welfare battle and the military battle. The military battle has an overall commander on either side and clear lines of command whereas the welfare battle is diffuse in organisation and leadership.

This feature of the welfare battle should not obscure the fact that the many individuals and groups involved in welfare rights do possess a vision of wider reforms and longer-term aims, and the tactical skirmishes do contribute towards larger ends. Those participants and supporters of welfare rights activities who condemn tactical successes and support an alternative society approach to social reform ignore the achievements of tactical processes in achieving large-scale changes in the welfare system. It is possible to present a cogent historical interpretation of progress in welfare which focuses on the vision of individual and groups' persuasive attrition over many years using all the political and professional means at their disposal. The contributions of the Fabian Society and the tradition of the Webbs give a testament for this approach.

The plurality of welfare rights organisations and the wide divergencies of attitude within them are simultaneously encouraging and depressing; encouraging by the admission that there are few simple answers to major social evils and many alternative supportive and complementary service elements may be needed to root out poverty, squalor and ignorance; depressing because the very honesty that this plurality reveals hinders the development of welfare rights as a social movement. As at no point since the cos became aware of the need for liaison and organisation in welfare, we see reforming movements dogged by the multiplicity of organisations and ineffective co-ordination.[30] Welfare rights groups are no exception. Organisations like Shelter, Child Poverty and Claimants Union seem sometimes to be more concerned about their own identity than about their overlapping purposes and the possibilities for co-ordination. Thus whilst the seeds of a welfare rights movement exist there are few signs of their germinating into more than a marginal force in changing the welfare system. American experience is not very much more encouraging even though national organisation is much stronger.[31] The major evaluative work on welfare rights in America points out the problems of organisation and that the main achievement in the 1960s was getting more people on the welfare rolls rather than changing the system.[32] Such criticism should not be taken as discouragement to welfare rights workers in this country. It emphasises rather the resistances to change and the magnitude and complexity of the problem areas they are dealing with, which call for more effort in this field rather than retreat.

To what extent does a welfare rights terminology sharpen our conception of social reform? First, it concentrates attention on the fact that a minimum aim is to ensure that existing welfare rights are used to the full, and that this should not be confused with arguments for extending welfare rights to meet new social problems or existing ones in a different way. Second, it can sharpen our perception of where present welfare patterns are failing to deal with the problems because of fundamental defects. Thus most welfare rights workers are not revolutionary or extreme left radicals. They are continuing the tradition of social reform that this country has embraced since the nineteenth century. This is all the more reason why statutory organisations and their workers should not fear to become involved in this range of activities by direct participation or encouraging others. A clearer recognition of the links between welfare rights and existing traditions of reform should reduce the ambivalence many people in the welfare field feel at present.

Research and welfare rights

The role which the welfare rights movement can play in social reform is illustrated by their work in the field of research. Areas of research coverage are:

1 Individual problem cases in which even when all the available welfare help is brought to bear it is blatantly insufficient.

2 Survey evidence of lack of take-up of benefits. Guidance about the attitudes of individuals or groups to particular benefits and services.

3 Evidence about individuals or groups who live in areas where welfare agencies do not fulfil their statutory responsibilities to provide sufficient services of adequate standard.

4 Evidence about the extent and efficiency of information and advice services.

5 Evidence about the attitudes of welfare officials and administrative processes (e.g. the operation of discretionary procedures).

Each of these areas of research has been important in the development of welfare in this country for many years. What makes them significant at present is the overall shift to means-tested welfare benefits during the Conservative administration. The reliance on selectivity in benefits has the consequence that far more people are having to apply for benefits for which eligibility requirements may be complicated.[33] A further consequence is an increased administrative pressure on welfare agency staffs (e.g. officials of the Supplementary Benefits Commission, local authority housing departments, education welfare services), where public accountability and lack of financial resources lead agencies and their officials to interpret eligibility requirements strictly, in order to balance supply and demand for benefits.[34] The present administration of welfare is a large-scale quasi-experiment in extended selectivity and a large part of the work of welfare rights organisations must be to provide an effective critique and monitoring of this experiment.

Since selective benefits if badly or harshly administered cause much individual suffering to those who are benefiting and to those marginally ineligible, social workers should be closely allied to any movement which is critically evaluating this administration. It is social workers who are at the end of the welfare road when all else fails. If they are to prevent themselves from becoming the ultimate justification for selectivity, the final solution to failure in other parts of the welfare system, they must join with welfare rights workers and beneficiaries in evaluating the web of transactions within the welfare system. It is no accident therefore that a significant minority of social workers are active members of welfare rights groups.

The emphasis on the research element in welfare rights activity has been heavily dependent on the leadership and stimulation of teachers of social administration, many of whom are also responsible for teaching social workers. Not surprisingly, welfare rights organisations themselves have been in turmoil contending with the new face of welfare in the early 1970s. Where should the main efforts be channelled? Towards mediation and advocacy, advice and information, community work or research? There are signs that the research element, which can be fed into national policy debates, is being considered a more important element in their activities than direct service. Yet this should not obscure the diversity of functions of welfare rights groups and the way in which these activities buttress each other.

The future

I have argued that, far from being a novelty, welfare rights thinking involves sharpening our perceptions of a number of linked activities which have their origins in traditional, but evolving approaches to welfare. The weight given to these various components depends on the nature of the welfare system at the time, and the attitudes of welfare rights organisers and workers to it. The resulting balance and tensions will shape the purpose, strategy and tactics of welfare rights organisations.

Social workers and their agencies are already involved in these activities in a fragmentary way. I have suggested that social work tradition and the place of social work in the welfare system imposes an obligation on social workers and social work agencies to concern themselves with and participate in these activities. The welfare rights movement is much more broadly based than social work, but social workers cannot but be drawn into alliance with other participants in this field because of their pivotal position in the welfare field. What then should be the long-term strategy of welfare rights workers, whether social workers or others? The fundamental long-term aim is to establish basic welfare rights and reform the welfare institutions with the allied purpose of increasing levels of benefit and improving the quality of other services. It is one of the weaknesses of developments in welfare rights that the main attention has been centred on social security and housing services whereas the approach is applicable in any welfare sector. In the housing sector a long-term aim must be to establish a right to housing with a much higher minimum standard than exists today. Equally in the education and health fields the wide variations in quality of provision are a challenge to welfare rights workers. Unless the approach is applied to the whole welfare system there is the danger that welfare rights workers themselves could slide into a new materialism which sees people only as objects into which to pour physical welfare resources. Where the physical resources are of an appallingly inadequate standard they demand attention, but other elements in welfare rights should not be ignored. The emergence and support of the beneficiary as an active human agent is a development which is awkward for professionals but may at least have the benefit of making them pause in the administration and planning of welfare.

The immediate tactics involve the further expansion of efforts to ensure full take-up of benefits—efficient information and advice systems, mediation and advocacy, improvements in administration —and the strengthening of the social work contribution in this area. So far the sporadic forays of social workers into this field of work within their agencies has been looked on with suspicion if not hostility. The reason for this seems clear from Figure 1.

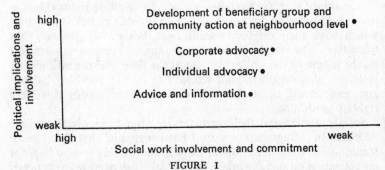

FIGURE 1

It is in those welfare rights activities which are viewed as having the strongest political implications and involvement, that there is the deepest suspicion from social workers and their organisations. This suspicion is misplaced. The range of activities which form the backbone of welfare rights work are clearly within existing law and are in the main attempting to ensure the equitable and efficient working of the law. To complain about such activities, because they demonstrate inadequacies which face professionals and politicians with difficult moral choices, seems illogical in the extreme in view of the fact that moral choice and conflict between competing practical alternatives are the basic stuff of political and professional life. Inevitably, social workers will experience conflict and tension over the degree and type of such involvement in welfare rights, but the involvement exists: today every social worker is a welfare rights worker on each occasion he advises an applicant to the social services department, refers someone to another welfare agency or supports BASW in a plan for improving family allowances or pensions.

However, if the welfare rights movement is to make a sufficient impact, problems of sponsorship, leadership and organisation will have to be overcome. Present developments are diffuse and patchy, and can hardly be called a social movement in this country. The reluctance to have strong formal patterns of organisation in many welfare rights bodies does reduce their power and authority at the national level, and these dilemmas of control and local organisation are still being worked out. One way of providing a firmer base out of which leadership and organisation can grow is through a growing contribution from social workers. They, amongst the professions, are the group with the widest knowledge of and most intimate daily contact with the welfare system, which should provide them with both the expertise and the enthusiasm.

Notes

1 H. Bosanquet, *Rich and Poor*, Macmillan, 1896, p. 181.
2 For an elegant discussion of the possible dangers of public welfare see J. C. Pringle's introductory statement for a session of the Third International Conference in Social Work. Le Play House Press, London, 1938, pp. 102-11. He gives a qualified judgment (p. 108): 'How far, therefore, the invasion of abstract collectivism and its concomitant bureaucracy—natural and perhaps inevitable in large urban aggregates of population, and under the relentless pressure of the exigencies of "politics"—has scarred the quality of the contacts arising in social service, and has *pro tanto* damaged community life, has not, as Fräulein von Arlt points out, been sufficiently investigated to admit of any finding upon it.'
3 It is interesting that R. Pinker, the author of one of the most acclaimed recent books in social administration—*Social Theory and Social Policy*, Heinemann, 1971—spends a great deal of time examining the nature and quality of the relationships involved in what Pringle would have called 'the social service contact'. Pringle and many of his fellow workers recognised that what happened in the social work contact could be a crucial criterion in evaluating the operation of social services. It is ironic that some sociologists should have just recently discovered that relationship is important whilst continuing to berate social workers who had grasped this fact much earlier.
4 If no radical thinking had emerged in the cities, social work would have been a very sponge-like profession. A high proportion of social workers are young and idealistic, they have a grounding in social services and they experience daily the extremes of injustice in our society. The profession should be grateful that some social workers at times refuse to be cogs in an administrative nightmare.
5 For a systematic discussion of the problems involved in the development and use of Social Indicators, see Andrew Shonfield and Stella Shaw (eds), *Social Indicators and Social Policy*, Heinemann, 1972.
6 See the paper 'Social Welfare as a Human Right' by Wayne Vasey, in *Social Work Values in an Age of Discontent*, Council on Social Work Education, 1970, pp. 76-86.
7 Tony Lynes discusses the nature of rights in the Supplementary Benefits Scheme in *The Penguin Guide to Supplementary Benefits*, 1972; see particularly pp. 19-21, 23-6. He clearly outlines the legal entitlements to benefits and the way in which administrative practice and discretion limit these. J. Heywood and B. Allen, in their study of financial discretion exercised by Children's Departments under the Children and Young Persons Act 1963,

showed much confusion and variations in practice. See their *Financial Help in Social Work*, Manchester University Press, 1971.

8 'A New Concept of Responsibility in Social Relations', pp. 67-75 in *Social Work Values in an Age of Discontent*, Council on Social Work Education, 1970.

9 The first British Local Welfare Rights booklet was published in Liverpool in 1968. In the Introduction to the Revised Edition, March 1969, the purpose is stated as follows: 'This booklet has been prepared as a means of encouraging more people on low incomes to make greater use of selective benefits.' See *Welfare Benefits, A Guide for Welfare Workers in Liverpool*, Revised Edition 1971, Liverpool Personal Service Society (Inc.).

10 For illuminating arguments about the importance of social workers in helping to use the public welfare system see Martin Rein, 'The cross-roads for social work', *Social Work Quarterly*, vol. 27, no. 4, October 1970. See also the discussion by F. Hollis in her chapter on Environmental Work in *Casework: A Psychosocial Therapy*, second edition, Random House, 1972, pp. 139-63.

11 R. Brooke gives the most recent picture of CAB services in *Information and Advice Services*, Bell, 1972. See also her article in *New Society*, 20 July 1972, 'Advice for citizens', in which she argues for a strengthening of CAB services. Government support is in fact being increased.

12 For accounts of the variety of pattern in Family Advice Centres see A. Leissner, *Family Advice Centres*, Longman, 1967; and A. Leissner K. A. M. Herdman, and E. O. Davies, *Advice, Guidance and Assistance*, Longman, 1971.

13 Under the Local Government Act (1972), local authorities have the power to levy up to 2p rate for such services but few do so.

14 Janet Streather, 'Welfare rights and the social worker', *Social Work Today*, vol. 3, no. 13, 5 October 1972.

15 O. Stevenson, *Claimant or Client*, Allen & Unwin 1973. She argues that better informed social workers will be able to understand and co-operate with SBC officials to get the best out of the system, as well as act as informed critics.

16 See chapters 8 and 9 of *Fifth Social Service*, Fabian Society, 1970; T. Lynes, 'Welfare Rights'; D. Bull, 'Action for Welfare Rights'.

17 A. S. Kahn *et al.*, *Neighbourhood Information Services*, Columbia School of Social Work, 1966.

18 The Supplementary Benefits Commission seems to rely widely on social workers to underpin a faulty system: 'They [the Commission] also attach great importance to improving the awareness of supplementary benefit claimants of the help that may be available, and to the part that social workers, voluntary bodies and others can play in encouraging them to make their essential needs known.' See 'Exceptional Needs Payments', *Supplementary Benefits Administration Papers*, no. 4, p. 23, HMSO, 1973.

19 See Rein, op. cit., also J. L. Ecklein and A. A. Lauffer, *Community Organisers and Social Planners*, Wiley, 1972. Chapter 4, 'The Organiser as man in the Middle', is particularly useful. Bull (op. cit.) discusses advocacy in the British context.

20 As in F. F. Piven and R. A. Cloward, *Regulating the Poor*, Pantheon Books, 1971. The thesis in their book would be supported by recent British experience. High unemployment in 1967-73 has been associated with an emphasis on repression and control in the Supplementary Benefits system and culminated in the setting up of the Fisher Committee in March 1971. There has been more concern with alleged abuse than with ensuring that all beneficiaries obtain full entitlement.

21 B. Wootton, *Social Science and Social Pathology*, Allen & Unwin, 1959.
22 R. Lubove, *The Professional Altruist*, Harvard University Press. R. Lubove sees the mediating, co-ordinating role as complementary to other kinds of social work help, whereas B. Wootton deprecates help with emotional problems as an avoidance and disguising of the real problem of poverty.
23 R. M. Titmuss was pessimistic about relying too heavily on a legalistic approach to welfare rights and he discussed the problem of a caselaw approach in American Welfare Rights programmes. See 'Welfare rights, law and discretion', *Political Quarterly*, April 1971, pp. 113-32.
24 For succinct discussion of these trends see, 'Popular Participation in Development: Emerging Trends in Community Development', UN, E.71, IV.2, 1971. The report outlines developments throughout the world and stresses the essential similarity of need, though for different reasons, for participation in advanced and developing countries.
25 The concept of 'beneficiary' is taken from Blau and Scott's classification of organisations. Even 'beneficiary' is value-laden in that it may be assumed that people benefit from service, which may not be the case. More neutral terms are 'user' and 'recipient'. See P. M. Blau and W. R. Scott, *Formal Organisations*, Routledge & Kegan Paul, 1967, pp. 51-4.
26 See the proposals for client involvement in R. Holman, *Socially Deprived Families in Britain*, Bedford Square Press, 1970, pp. 198-9.
27 A much more flexible approach to the use of co-option of beneficiaries on department working parties and sub-committees could be of the greatest value.
28 The major British studies are referred to in *The Social Planning of Urban Renewal*, North West Economic Planning Council, September 1972. See also Shonfield and Shaw (eds), op. cit.
29 See the valuable discussion by G. Popplestone, 'Collective action among private tenants', *British Journal of Social Work*, vol. 2, no. 3, Autumn 1972, pp. 369ff; 'The ideology of professional community workers', *British Journal of Social Work*, vol. 1, no. 1, April 1971.
30 In 1972, 2,219 charities were registered, 1,006 of which were founded in 1972. At 31 December 1972 over 100,000 charities were registered with the Charity Commissioner. See *Report of the Charity Commissioners for England and Wales for the year 1972*, HMSO, 1973.
31 R. Holman gives a good picture of the American Welfare Rights movement in 'Changes in American welfare rights', *New Society*, vol. 21, no. 520, 21 September 1972. See also E. James, *America Against Poverty*, Routledge & Kegan Paul, 1970.
32 Piven and Cloward, op. cit.
33 The number of applications under the Supplementary Benefits scheme rose from 6,081,000 in 1968 to 6,424,000 in 1971. In the same period 'exceptional circumstances additions' fell from 527,000 to 425,006, whilst single payments for exceptional needs increased from 470,000 to 576,000.
34 The effects of inadequate staffing are commented on by the Fisher Committee who found that in supplementary benefits examined by the auditors in 1971, wrong assessments were found in 7.3 per cent of regular weekly cases and 9.3 per cent of immediate payments, about half of which were estimated to be underpayments. *Report of the Committee on Abuse of Social Security Benefits*, HMSO, 1973, p. 231. If these figures are representative this means that it is likely that approximately 100,000 weekly beneficiaries are being underpaid (1971). Compare this with the annual rate of appeals—21,000-22,000.

8

New Careers: power sharing in social work

Philip Priestley

Snakes and ladders

Interpreting real-life situations in terms of games, with players' roles and rules of play, can be as Berne has shown, not only amusingly diverting but solidly instructive as well.[1]

Status mobility in modern industrial society, for example, can be conceptualised as a game of snakes and ladders. The ladders are self explanatory and represent well-marked routes to fame and fortune. A few of them rise precipitously from near the bottom of the board to the top. Lucky individuals mount these ladders with the help of sudden literary success, windfall accessions of wealth or once-in-a-lifetime technical or commercial innovations. And for a few people, marriage can mean instant increments of money and class.

For most people, however, access is only possible to a different set of shorter ladders which together constitute the educational system. These ladders are discontinuous and entry to successive stages is progressively restricted; nominally by standards of intelligence and academic attainment, but in practice by class and cultural barriers which favour those who start off from already quite elevated positions in the game. Education is the principal mechanism in our society for permitting and regulating the flow of upward mobility and it faithfully mirrors the most salient aspects of the social order it serves. Successful performers in the educational game are rewarded with status, income and power.

Conversely, the people who fail to make headway up the educational pyramid are losers, consigned to their lowly stations in life without hope of escape. They tend to be the children of the poor, the dispossessed and the disadvantaged who are locked in the currently fashionable, so-called 'cycle of deprivation'.[2] To them can be added numbers of other individuals, not necessarily born to poverty or powerlessness, but delivered into those conditions by social processes which have the opposite effects to those of education.

These are the snakes of the game—a variety of institutionalised arrangements which exist for the purpose of *removing* status, income and power from people. Mental health, corrections and income maintenance schemes may all be superficially designated as services, but their receipt invariably contains major elements of personal degradation. Commentators such as Garfinkel[3] have catalogued and analysed some of these processes as 'ceremonies' which mark a downward status passage for the luckless participant. And Goffman[4] has elaborated the idea of a 'moral career' to describe the stabilisation of individual roles at new, lower levels. A wider explanation of the phenomenon has been proposed by Erikson[5] who suggests the utility of demotion for the maintenance of social group boundaries, whatever the damage to the individuals involved. Despite the widespread currency of these ideas, and those of the 'deviance' school, amongst social workers, they have led to remarkably little practical action designed to mitigate the destructive personal impact of the demotion process. Nor have they prompted social workers to construct realistic escape routes from the terminal roles which many of them help to administer; such as permanent inmate, ex-mental patient or parolee. So far as one can tell from talking to social workers, the view seems to be abroad that a simple awareness of the 'labelling' perspective is enough to ward off the worst of its supposed consequences. Unhappily for the afflicted client, this talismanic faith in the power of pure knowledge persists in the face of its proven ineffectiveness.

A concrete example of what might be attempted can be taken from the situation which faces the man leaving prison. A major part of the difficulty he has in resuming his place in society is the seemingly irrevocable nature of the spoiled identity conferred on him originally by the court and confirmed subsequently by the experience of imprisonment. Even though the length of his sentence may have been calculated so as to express the extent of his 'debt to society', and the serving of it construed as its repayment, the discharged prisoner will still find that the stigma lingers on.[6] Caught between deceit and despair, the most that the average ex-prisoner can hope for is that as time passes the stain on his name will fade and finally disappear. No one yet appears to have thought of accelerating the snail's-pace progression by formulating and enacting ceremonies for the *restoration* of status.

To the general rule of creative inertia in this direction in recent years there is a singular and startling exception—New Careers.

New Careers

No attempt will be made in this account to give in detail the past development and present achievements of the New Careers movement in the USA. That ground is well covered elsewhere.[7] Instead, we will examine its claims to mark a radical new departure in social work with revolutionary implications for the position of the client and the power to transform traditional agency organisation and practice.

The philosophy of New Careers is a curious blend of Samuel Smiles[8] and Cloward and Ohlin.[9] On the one hand, it runs, there exists in all modern urban societies, a large pool of socially and economically disadvantaged people. Although exposed, to the same extent as everyone else, to an incessant incitement to the possession and consumption of goods and services, they are denied at almost every turn any legitimate access to them. Lack of work explains their fundamental poverty and underlies a further deprivation; the dispossession of role which chronic unemployment brings with it. Additionally they suffer from a set of interlocking, multiple handicaps in the areas of health, motivation, language, education and technical skills. To the disadvantaged person there is no obvious way out of this Chinese-puzzle assembly of problems.

On the other hand, the argument continues, the agencies through which society claims to deal with health, education or welfare problems—the 'human services'—all suffer from chronic manpower shortages. Thus hampered, they fail to deliver more than token levels of service to their target populations. In neither quantity nor quality do they come anywhere near the level of effort necessary to lift men and women out of poverty and misery and into economic sufficiency and social dignity.

The answer to both problems, it is concluded, with barely concealed glee, is to recruit the poor to work in the helping agencies. It is a simple and audacious concept, blessed as such ideas often are, with the surface brilliance of paradox. It also brings with it a train of powerful supporting propositions which have to do with the nature of the whole social work enterprise, and its methods of personnel recruitment and training. And between them they raise a harvest of thorny questions which social workers have managed to shelve during their long pursuit of professionalism.

The origins of ideas and particularly those which lead to social action are notoriously difficult to trace and New Careers is no exception. But it is possible to distinguish four major contributory factors in its development into a movement which now claims the creation of close on half a million new jobs in the USA. One of them is political, two are theoretical and the last practical.

Politically the roots of the notion go back to the long hot summers of the late 1950s and early 1960s when, one after the other, large American city ghettoes went off like a string of fire-crackers. Trapped, almost literally, in decaying inner-city slums and ignored by consensus politicians too busy peddling the good life elsewhere, the new poor had finally risen in a blind fury. At the time the cop-stoning, fire-raising, store-looting mobs must have looked to the forces of law and order like the advance guard of more general disorder. In the immediate aftermath of violence some time-honoured American remedies were applied. Money was rushed to the scene. Work, or the lack of it, was identified early on as the main culprit and a lot of the cash was channelled into crash training programmes to fit people into existing jobs and into the creation of additional jobs along old New Deal lines. The trouble was that the new poor were not the New Deal poor. Their numbers were not so much a function of low demand and stagnant produc-tion, as a measure of technological efficiency in a generally buoyant economy. They were, and are, in fact, the structurally unemployed. The answer to their problem therefore did not lie with a Keynesian application of public works in the old style, but with a strategy that followed the drift of the labour market away from production and towards the service sector.[10] The New Careers formulation fitted that particular bill at a time when massive federal funding[11] became available to implement it on a scale that matched the boldness of its conception.

Cloward and Ohlin's contribution on the theoretical side has already been referred to.[12] It follows from their theory of blocked aspirations that some way has to be found, not simply of giving more money to poor people but of providing dignified and legiti-mate life-styles around which its expenditure can be organised. Stigma cannot just be bought off and the cumulative effects of generations spent in the ghetto will not fall away overnight because a Bill has been passed in Congress.

The bootstrap virtues of Samuel Smiles appear again at this junc-ture in a strange alliance with Donald Cressey[13] and his extended version of the theory of differential association. In its original form Sutherland[14] had asserted that criminal behaviour is learned by individuals who mix with others whose values appear to 'legitimate' delinquent activities. Cressey has inferred from the theory a pos-sible method of resocialisation, that is by arranging for habitual offenders to mix with others who do *not* continually affirm the rightness of their offensive activities but who pursue collectively more socially acceptable aims.

Examples of the principle in action are provided by numerous self-help groups of which Alcoholics Anonymous and Synanon are the best known. They are part of a vigorous tradition which has furnished some practical models for the emergent idea of New

Careers. One of the achievements of AA, for instance, has been the transformation of the 'drunkard' into the 'recovering alcoholic' not only in his own eyes but those of his family and parts of the wider society as well. An acceptable self-conception and a publicly presentable persona may be vital prerequisites for individual advancement but they contain in themselves no prescriptions for worldly success.

Declaring a bad past is one way of trying to ensure a better present—what New Careers adds to that is exactly what its title says—the notion of a future 'career'. Ex-prisoners and recovering alcoholics can spend a lot of time helping each other and helping themselves in the process, but they must normally earn their bread and butter in a work-world which is totally divorced from those activities. And even when they have managed to find full-time jobs in a related field these have tended to be low-order, low-pay positions which lead precisely nowhere. Hospital porters or assistant wardens in alcoholic or ex-prisoner hostels are often employed to do the dirty work so as to free the 'professional' staff to pursue more glamorous 'treatment' activities.

New Careers, on the other hand, starts by analysing the tasks which are performed by doctors, teachers and social workers. Critically assessed, many of their specific functions appear to require neither the lengthy training and supposed skill of the professional, nor the rate of reward which their practice presently commands. Some of these activities can clearly be hived off and reconstructed to form aide or sub-professional roles. These roles in turn can be filled and competently performed by quite ordinary people, given brief but adequate training and relevant supervision. And *extraordinary* people like ex-prisoners and chronic unemployees can bring to their performance of such roles a unique dimension of personal experience and understanding from the inside of the problems they have to deal with.

Classroom aides for example can organise and manage teaching materials, keep records and administer a whole range of other non-teaching activities. Health aides can encourage service take-up by target group members, engage in public education projects and carry out routine medical testing. Probation aides can help parolees and probationers to find accommodation, get work and negotiate initial payments from income maintenance agencies.

The fact that the aides are black, live in ghettoes or have themselves been prisoners is necessary to the New Careers scheme of things, but not in itself sufficient to constitute the full programme. For that, there must also be opportunities for further training, access to progressively more skilled posts with higher statuses and salaries and eventual entry into the full professional grades of the service on equal terms with more conventionally recruited members.[15]

The general promise of New Careers can therefore be summed up under the following six heads, which will also form the basis of a consideration of its prospects for implementation in this country:

1 Income for the poor.
2 Work for the 'unemployable'.
3 Status escalation for the stigmatised.
4 Manpower for the 'human' services.
5 Qualitative transformation of social work.
6 A revolution in training design and method.

It is an ambitious list to say the least—in fact a precis programme for the redistribution of status, power and wealth. The first question that should be asked is why the idea has taken so long to cross the Atlantic. In the ten years since its inception, an enormous and diversified movement has grown up in the USA. The first small-scale projects, based on its principles, are only now being set up here.[16]

Funding is probably the most crucial element in the successful implementation of New Careers. It was the violence of the 'urban crisis' which struck loud responsive chords on the American public purse-strings. Similar conditions do exist here, but not of the scale and degree which preceded the explosion there. The British way with ghettoes has been the bulldozer and the partial dispersement of problem families on to new housing estates distantly sited beyond suburbia. The advent of large immigrant communities, a rapidly obsolescent housing stock and an intensified sense of relative poverty, as general standards of living reach ever higher levels, may lead in time to equivalent disorders on British city streets; but if and until they do, any widespread local adoption of the idea seems improbable. And in the absence of an official political constituency, driven forward by a fuel of high-octane fear, from where else should one expect the demand to provide the resources for New Careers to take root and grow? Obviously not from mainstream social work where the vested interests of 'professionalism' and 'conservative' local control converge in solid resistance to the role of prime mover in such a matter.[17] Nor from the radical forces inside social work. Few in number, poorly organised, ideologically incoherent and lacking experience of changing anything, they are an unlikely source of irresistible pressure on the establishment.[18]

Clearly the natural constituency for New Careers lies amongst the poor and the dispossessed themselves; the 'clientele' of social work in other words. Which leads to one of the central difficulties of the entire idea, the question of its authorship. Movements like

AA and Synanon and the home-grown Preservation of the Rights of Prisoners (PROP) all arose directly and spontaneously out of the experiences of their members as alcoholics, junkies or time-serving prisoners. The solutions which they propose to their problems are all their own work and their own responsibility; as are their successes and their failures. In one sense they succeed only to the extent that they reject what middle-class theorists and social pathologists have told them about themselves. Recent developments have made this a more difficult thing to do, since even the protests of the poor against the repressive parts of the welfare system have been insidiously colonised by the chic radicalism of the PR pressure groups. The rhetoric of dissent is now provided ready-wrapped by a new breed of articulate and professionally angry young men. Prisoners have a good word for do-gooders of this kind, even those who purport to take their side against authority, but who make a good living at it. They describe them as 'poncing off crime'. 'Poncing off' poverty, homelessness, mental health, crime, homosexuality and old age now provides attractive career opportunities for bright young graduates in sociology and social administration who are infected with the view that all social work is the velvet glove around the iron fist of state repression. When the poor or the stigmatised wish to make their own points in their own way, the new professionals resent the refusal to recognise the superior effectiveness of their own propaganda and media-manipulation. Relations between Claimants' Unions and Child Poverty Action Groups illustrate the rift which exists between the indigenous and the professional protesters in a particular area of social policy. And the collapse in 1972 of PROP's summer season of prison riots was accompanied by a chorus of 'Told you so's' from deliberately excluded academics and penal reformers.[19]

To summarise: one of the preconditions for success is that New Careers, despite its 'professional' and theoretical origins, should accurately reflect in practice the concerns and aspirations of the people whom it now designates, not as a target clientele but as a potential source of social work personnel.

The New Careerist

For the individual New Careerist this shift in definition and the transition of identity from 'client' to worker has profound implications. But how do the changes in his life measure up to the first three items of the six-point summary enumerated earlier, namely income, work and status?

So far as income is concerned the immediate answer seems to be that he will get more money as an entry-grade New Careerist than as a recipient of the dole—but only just.[20] Marginally better than bread-line wage rates may make sense to hesitant employers uncertain as to the value they can place on the labours of their new recruits. They make even more sense to State financiers who get a day's work out of the poor in return for a payment which barely exceeds what they were previously given to remain idle. But they make a nonsense of New Careers' claim to be more than an updated version of poorhouse make-work. Picking oakum and visiting the sick have quite a lot in common if they are exacted in return for a grudgingly given minimum income.

Satisfactory pay, in the end, must depend on the ability of the new employees to demonstrate that what they do makes a useful and otherwise unobtainable contribution to the work of an agency. Improved communications with client groups and their host communities, increased take-up of services, a heightened tempo of innovation; gains like these in agency performance can be used to press the case for higher pay.

Precedents in this country, however, for mounting such a campaign are not promising. There exists here already, in social work, a vast army of unskilled, untrained and poorly paid operatives. They work mainly in the residential sector, in children's and old people's homes, reception and assessment centres, colonies and hospitals for the mentally handicapped, psychiatric hospitals, hostels and correctional establishments for children. They are the warehousemen of the social services, charged with the daily management and maintenance of an enormous population of the 'put-away'. Here, more than amongst the unemployed poor, is a primary untapped source of pressure for change, although whether the 'keepers' would willingly forge an alliance with the people they 'mind' is doubtful. At all events, they find themselves in occupational blindalleys which New Careers must transform if it is to move on.

Some of the same strictures apply to the allied question of status. It is true that in the USA there have been spectacular successes. Of Douglas Grant's original eighteen trainees in a Californian prison, only one went back inside and many of the remainder have landed high-pay, high-ranking jobs as programme heads and advisers.[21] One of them is responsible for an official plan virtually to dismantle the use of custody for young offenders in Massachusetts. And there is no doubt that social work is a rising star in the occupational firmament. But status has traditionally rested on exclusivity. New Careers, by contrast, calls for the breaking down of barriers and the opening up of entry to the professional ranks in a wholesale way. Might not one consequence of success in this respect be an actual diminution of the status of the jobs to which access has been created? Even less attractive, might not the individual's achievement of high status in social work lead to the attrition of the very quality which took him there, namely his identification with the client?

Apart from what happens to a particular aspirant in New Careers, his rise does have a wider significance for the people he leaves behind. Whether they can follow his example or not, his former peers in adversity experience an expansion of their financial horizons. They also see new possibilities of 'moral progress' towards equality and acceptance. Well-publicised success stories by minority group members should in theory affect majority attitudes towards the whole group.[22] In status terms therefore the balance of the account appears to be reasonably favourable.

As a cure however, on any scale, for unemployment there are a number of qualifying factors. Some of them are possibly special to the British situation but they are critical to any assessment of the movement's chances here.

First, there is the size and complexion of the respective unemployment populations. Gross unemployment figures in Britain, although subject to severe fluctuations, revert constantly to a position around the 2 per cent mark.[23] In the USA it is nearer 5 per cent. A markedly different attitude to productivity is concealed in the gap between the two rates. In some industries the average American worker, using similar amounts of capital equipment, achieves a rate of output exactly twice that of his British counterpart.[24] In other words some industries here are double manned. Or put another way, in Britain the available work is more widely spread amongst the available work force.[25] As a result the ranks of the British unemployed are not necessarily filled with suitable candidates for posts as social workers or other human services aides. Nor, for obvious reasons, does the unemployment total contain such disproportionate representation of black or brown immigrant groups as in the USA.

Second, it must be asked how attractive a job in human services would be to members of a working-class culture that gives great respect to the acquisition and exercise of manual crafts, trades and skills. New Careers does not speak to this tradition at all.

Third, given the selectivity which is essential for the provision of acceptable services by trainees, there must be considerable doubt about the ability of even quite major programmes to absorb more than a tiny fraction of the currently unemployed.

On all these grounds it is necessary to speak with some reserve about the chances of large-scale implementation of New Careers in this country. At the same time, there are compelling arguments for its introduction; not so much because of its effect on the individuals involved but for its potential as a transforming agent of the power relationships which characterise the contemporary social work scene.

Power

Power is not a word that springs lightly to the lips of most social workers. A trained incapacity to think in terms wider than the unique, individual 'case' and a narrow concern for the outwardly visible signs of a profession have left them untroubled by what might be called the politics of altruism.

In the remainder of this discussion some of the sources of power in social work will be identified and a mechanism suggested through which New Careers could be used to re-order some of the unequal relationships that flow from them.

The sources include central policy-making, local political control, legal sanctions, hierarchical organisation, professionalism and the use of information. The list is not exhaustive and is not arranged in any real order of priority. Nor does it include a preliminary query about one of the basic symptoms of power in all organisations: the ability to secure resources, not merely to meet present requirements, but to sustain future growth as well. One of the major assumptions of New Careers' theorists is that 'human services' are a high growth industry. On past showing they are probably right but it is not an assumption that should be made unthinkingly or accepted uncritically. Definitions of welfare needs are almost infinitely extendible; provision inevitably limps along behind a tide of rising expectations, and pressure groups make daily demands for more expenditure. Like growth economics, growth welfare is an unquestionable article of faith; indeed the two are probably inseparable.

The alternative, which is never discussed, is that welfare agencies should so direct their efforts that they lead to the eventual 'withering away of social work'. The reason for the rude-noise status of this notion in polite welfare circles rests firmly on a developed sense of self-preservation and an equal reluctance to contemplate the transfer of power to the community which it entails.

In the meantime we are left with a slightly surrealist vision of New Careerists pursuing their own problems in ever decreasing circles and finally disappearing, with wild cries, up their own Seebohms.

Of all the obstacles that confront the idea of New Careers none can equal the subtlety and strength of 'professionalism'. The strongest of its assets is the unreasoning nature of its appeal. Professionalism rests on what people 'know' or 'feel in their bones' and which stimulates instinctive responses, particularly in situations of danger. In the presence of a client who wishes to become a worker, these reflexes instruct social workers to close ranks. After all, it has taken them generations to achieve what is still only a semi-professional position, and now even these slender gains are threatened by the new thinking.

It would be mischievous to suggest that social workers have an obsession with status but the features of something which resembles it are embedded in their everyday practices. Physical arrangements are used to emphasise the different roles of the actors. Desks are used as barriers and metaphorical buttresses. There is the language of the chairs. Workers' chairs have arms, clients' do not. Or clients are given easy chairs which leave the worker in a higher position. Slum waiting rooms. Derelict lavatories or no lavatories for clients; signless and locked lavatories for staff.[27] The non-reciprocal use of christian names.

The fact that many social workers are upwardly mobile members of the lower middle class may explain as much of this as 'professionalism', but in actual interaction with 'clients' both factors are operative. One need not accept more than a part of what Bernstein[28] has to say about class codes of speech to appreciate the difficulties of cross-class communication in this country.[29] And it needs no linguistic theory at all to recognise that social work language serves an essentially mystifying function.[30] Frequently the arcane mysteries to which it alludes are so complex, ill-formulated and eclectically held that the jargon itself is the only common ground between practitioners. In an interview situation where one of the participants operates according to the rules of a deeply-rooted implicit theory about the encounter, there is an immediate imbalance of power. The imbalance derives from the special knowledge of the worker, or more accurately from his special beliefs, since what he 'knows' or claims to 'know' is a heterogeneous mixture of 'facts' and values handed out to him during his professional socialisation. None of this 'knowledge', not even the relevant part of it, is communicated, i.e. is made explicit, to the client, who has no opportunity to agree or disagree with its basic assumptions or to organise the business of the meeting around his own agenda.

Training methods for New Careers suggest a method of redistributing power in this, the basic micro-situation of social work. The methods are based on the premise that the technical content of social work knowledge—human growth and development, social administration, theories of deviance, etc.—can all be imparted to the untutored and academically inexperienced trainee, if they are first of all suitably translated and then immediately related to practical tasks.[31] A wider and equally fruitful field for such 'translations' would be to make the same material accessible to clients in the same way. Shared knowledge reduces the ability of one party in two-party proceedings to manipulate the other, without his being aware of it. Shared knowledge makes a beginning towards the equalisation of power within the worker–client relationship. New Careerists are the people to help with the 'translations' and with interpreting them as part of a wider public education. If one effect of their work was to warn clients that simple requests for material help were liable to be interpreted as symbolic cries for help with 'underlying' disorders, it would provoke refreshing gales of laughter and be followed, hopefully, by massive abstentions from the client role.

Even when the value of worker-clients is admitted by the professionals there is one remaining reticence. Social workers clutch at 'confidentiality' as the last fig-leaf protecting their professional virtue. As a pure principle it is to be applauded, but its actual interpretation is a curious one. It consists of keeping files and case-notes to which literally hundreds of other social workers and hired clerical hands have access, but which are kept secret from the client. The presence of New Careerists alert to libels and misrepresentations could help to reverse that situation into something like its rightful form; which is that case files should be 'open' between client and worker and 'closed' to everybody else.

There are problems too in the lower reaches of 'professionalism' namely the staff cultures which exist in institutions. My own experience in a prison is instructive. When, as a welfare officer, I 'employed' a serving prisoner as a full-time research and editorial assistant in the compilation and publication of a guide to the job market for ex-prisoners,[32] prison officers responded in a strange way. They did not mind so much the idleness, as they saw it, of a man sitting in a cell all day and not sewing mailbags or stripping cable. What they did resent was the new identity which the work gave to the man involved. A part of his task was to canvass by post large numbers of employers, unions, trade and professional associations. One batch of replies to such a mailing was consistently defaced by the duty censor officer for the day who scored out every 'Mr' in letters which began 'Dear Mr —'.

Prisoners of course are numbers and surnames and the touchiness about honorifics is a stronger version of the distinctions which social workers draw between themselves and their customers. And both are extensions of the divisions which exist in the internal organisation of institutional and social work staffs themselves. Hierarchical power is something over which workers and clients alike exercise little control; in the case of the client, he never even comes face to face with other than its lowest strata. Towards the principle of hierarchy, the New Careers philosophy is ambivalent.

At first blush it appears to attack the exclusiveness of entry by credentials to the premier grades of the profession. It proposes to replace them with an open-ended system of entry in which aptitude and experience count for as much as college credits and diplomas. But from there on the new entrant must rise by merit, on terms almost identical to those now in existence.

It is a pity that no attempt has yet been made to apply the New Careers job analyses of basic grade 'helper' positions to those of the higher echelons. At the lower levels it is possible to disentangle many of the constituent elements of the role and to demonstrate the ease with which they can be taught to men and women who are recruited straight off the streets. Might not a similar picture emerge if supervisory and chief executive positions were subjected to the same scrutiny? It is difficult to suppress a sneaking suspicion that the principal role of agency heads in the 'human services' is to answer the telephone if anyone 'important' calls. Further aspects of their work—calling meetings, developing policy, reporting to committees, ensuring that work is allocated and done—could all be performed equally well if distributed amongst the ordinarily competent members of the basic grade staff. Even when the tasks demand experience, judgment or flair, there is no reason why those who possess these qualities should not contribute them within the framework of a collective endeavour.

American New Careerists, who are already advancing along the road of unionisation, have begun to treat the hierarchy issue as a live one.[33] The outcome of their debate could have consequences that will reverberate far beyond the boundaries of social work.

To stay true to the intentions of its creators, New Careers really needs to be institutionalised in a special way. However dramatic its initial impact on an employing agency there will inevitably follow a process of mutual accommodation that will erode its continuing effectiveness. An alternative model, which would exploit the special quality of New Careerists, without diminishing their integrity, would be the establishment of consumer protection offices for the users of the social services. Wholly staffed by 'indigenous' workers, their job would be to monitor the operations of the 'human services' and to exercise what amounts to a quality control function over them. Interposed between the agencies and their publics they could also research community and individual needs and communicate them to the responsible bodies. They could arbitrate in complaints by clients against services, provide advocacy services at tribunal hearings or on the McKenzie lawyer principle in the criminal courts, and advise prospective clients of their rights and the best sources of help with their particular problems. The worker's role in a consumer protection office would be an attractive and satisfying one to many 'indigenous' leaders who would baulk at being 'bought off' by the offer of official positions. Aide posts in the office would permit new entrants to test out the role and to move into permanent jobs either there or as mainstream social work New Careerists. The need for client protection is especially pronounced now that the Seebohm reorganisation has created a virtual monopoly situation in the supply of social work, along with new, all-time low standards of service in places.

But besides taking the poor on to the staff, or providing the means for consumer protection, there are more direct ways of sharing power with disadvantaged communities.

One of them is to give places to the poor on controlling committees, in numbers sufficient to have real impact on their decisions. Representation in penny numbers is not enough. It tends to promote either an Uncle Tom mentality or hopeless and ineffective anger. Substantial membership, say one-third of the total committee, gives the client group a solid base from which to make alliances or to hold a balance of power between competing factions. The appointment of establishment-minded members can be avoided by making their positions elective, either by area or by client-group constituencies. Passing reference in the Seebohm Report to client representation on committees has, not surprisingly, been passed over in silence, whilst the opportunities for creating wondrous hierarchies of high-paid posts have been seized with both hands.

An even more direct way of sharing power is simply to hand over control of an area social services team to the area it is supposed to serve. An elective community committee with a free hand to write policy might produce some interesting new directions for locally-based social work. At the same time it introduces the idea of the political rather than the paid New Careerist.

Marcuse[34] has identified the black, the poor and the stigmatised, i.e. the non-working classes, as the last islands of disorganisation in our over-organised consumer civilisation, and the only likely source of future resistance to the total triumph of technology over the free spirit of man. New Careers in its present nascent state offers both a promise and a threat to these groups. Within it can be discerned the seeds of a social and political transformation by peaceful means. Or as it develops, it may seduce and co-opt the potential leadership of the outsiders and institutionalise their critical functions into an impotent form of loyal opposition.

However it turns out, the odds could be equalised at the outset by injecting the whole debate, together with its principal actors, directly into the political arena. New Careerists would make fine political activists, keen lobby correspondents for community newspapers, adventurous investigators for the Ombudsman, able research assistants for busy MPs, or even Liberal MPs.

If, in the process, New Careers was consumed like a meteor striking the atmosphere, it would still leave as its lasting memorial an illumination of the indivisibility of social work and politics.

Notes

1 Eric Berne, *Games People Play*, André Deutsch, London, 1966.

2 Mrs Mia Kellmer-Pringle of the National Children's Bureau was commissioned by the DHSS during 1973 to spend six months in finding the answer to this problem.

3 Harold Garfinkel, 'Conditions of successful degradation ceremonies', *American Journal of Sociology*, 61, March 1956.

4 Erving Goffman, *Asylums*, Anchor Books, New York, 1961.

5 Kai Erikson, *Wayward Puritans*, Wiley, New York, 1966.

6 See for example the annual reports of the Apex Trust, which offers a specialist employment service to ex-prisoners, 2 Manchester Square, London, W.1.

7 Nancy Hodgkin, 'The New Careers project at Vacaville', *Howard Journal*, 13, 3, 1972; Dennie Briggs, *Dealing with Delinquents*, Hogarth, London, 1972.

8 Samuel Smiles, *Self Help*, 1859.

9 Richard Cloward and Lloyd Ohlin, *Delinquency and Opportunity*, Free Press, New York, 1960.

10 Department of Employment Gazette.

11 Under the Economic Opportunity Act (1964).

12 Cloward and Ohlin, op. cit.

13 Donald Cressey, 'Changing criminals; the application of the theory of differential association', *American Journal of Sociology*, 61, September 1955.

14 Edwin Sutherland, *Principles of Criminology*, J. B. Lippincott Co., Philadelphia, 1947.

15 Arthur Pearl and Frank Riessman, *New Careers for the Poor*, Free Press, New York, 1965.

16 The National Association for the Care and Resettlement of Offenders initiated in 1973 a pilot scheme in Bristol to train boys, who would otherwise be in Borstal, to become social work aides. Its annual output will be around twenty trainees.

17 Major innovations in British social work have rarely originated within its ranks.

18 Case-Con and the Islington barricades are its only fruits so far.

19 The Swedish equivalent, called KRUM, has from its inception been an alliance of radical professionals and ex-prisoners. It has been more successful in establishing a negotiating position with the prison authorities there but just as unsuccessful in achieving fundamental changes in the system.

20 The literature published by the New Careers Development Centre, New York University, refers to constant battles to raise the basic pay of entry grade New Careerists.

21 Hodgkin, op. cit.

22 Erving Goffman, *Stigma*, Prentice-Hall, Englewood Cliffs, New Jersey, 1963.

23 Department of Employment Gazette.

24 These disparities form a constant theme in the writings of American economist Walter Allen.

25 This is probably more cost-effective than either creating new jobs, or bearing the hidden costs of unemployment such as increased crime or other indicators of morbidity.

26 Local authority expenditure on social services more than doubled during the decade 1960-9.

27 I am indebted to Mervyn Murch for this insight.

28 Basil Bernstein, *Class, Codes and Control*, Routledge & Kegan Paul, London, 1971.

29 For a penetrating critique of the Bernstein thesis, see Harold Rosen, *Language and Class*, Falling Wall Press, Bristol, 1972.

30 Barbara Wootton, *Social Science and Social Policy*, Allen & Unwin, London, 1959.

31 Michael James and Edmond Lester, 'Training issues in implementing the use of the offender as a correctional manpower resource. Workshop proceedings. The offender as a correctional manpower resource. Institute for the Study of Crime and Delinquency, Asilomar, California, 1966.

32 *New Careers, A Handbook of Training and Employment Opportunities for Prisoners and Ex-prisoners*, Pillory Press, Cheltenham, 1972.

33 New Careers Newsletters, NCDC, New York University.

34 Herbert Marcuse, *One-dimensional Man*, Routledge & Kegan Paul, 1964.

9

The politics of behavior therapy:
the new cool-out casework? *

Irwin Epstein

Less than ten years ago, Richard Cloward and I described private
social welfare's disengagement from the American poor.[1] In that
paper we argued that professional caseworkers had adopted a
psychiatric technology which was ill-suited to the real environmental and material problems and problem-definitions of low-
income people. The consequence of this conflict between middle-
class professional technology and low-income culture was a decrease
in the provision of material and psychological services to poor
people.

Typically, social work agencies explained this disengagement in
conservative terms, suggesting that the problem was with the
poor themselves and their tendency to 'project' their psychological
problems into the environment. Adams and McDonald, in their
paper on 'clinical cooling out' of the poor, described the way in
which caseworkers convinced these clients to accept their fate as
'untreatable.'[2]

Today, many social workers are turning away from psychoanalytic psychiatry and toward behaviorism for their model of
casework practice. Skinner is replacing Freud as the totemic father
of social work. Predictably, questions have been raised in the social
work literature about the desirability of this trend. However, neither
critics nor proponents of the behavioral approach in social work
have fully considered the political and organizational implications
of behavioral practice with the poor, the involuntary client, and
other members of the political underclass. Advantages and dis-
advantages, uses and abuses of this new treatment technology are
discussed in a political and organizational vacuum. When considered, political problems are summarily dismissed as apolitical
issues of 'professional ethics.'[3] And organizational distortions of
practice are treated as idiosyncratic.

* Paper presented at the Symposium on Political Deviance, University
College, Cardiff, Wales, 14 November 1971.

But, in fact, social workers and their clients are rooted in the socio-political structure of the larger society and each therapeutic technology contains its own tacit political images of therapist, client, and their relation to the larger society.[4] Moreover, whatever its theoretical underpinnings, social work is practiced primarily within an organizational context, i.e. family service agencies, child guidance clinics, schools, mental hospitals, prisons, etc. As a result organizational influences on practice are inevitable.

The purpose of this paper is to consider critically some political and organizational aspects of behavioral practice by social workers. My basic thesis is that behavior therapy—as it is practiced by social workers with the poor, the involuntary client, and other members of the political underclass, e.g. women, children, mental defectives, homosexuals, etc.—can be as conservative and élitist a therapeutic technology as was the earlier psychoanalytic approach to casework.

It should be stated explicitly however that this analysis does not assume that behavioral methods are universally and inevitably used to retard social change or to reinforce the *status quo*. We simply do not know. There are no sociological studies of behavioral practice. Admittedly, the behavior therapy literature is a poor source of descriptive data, subject to various kinds of distortion. Published studies are never representative of the universe of practice. Successful treatment is more likely to be written about and published than is failure. Blatant abuses are covered up. Despite these difficulties, a selective review of the literature,[5] contact with behavioral programs and conversations with practitioners do suggest a number of important issues for further exploration.

It should be stated as well that this paper is not meant as a blanket condemnation of the behavioral approach. Indeed, the behavioral emphasis on specification of treatment goals and empirical assessment of their attainment makes behavior therapy potentially more effective, efficient and less duplicitous than other therapeutic technologies. In fact, it is this very specification of goals and means which makes the present analysis possible. In addition, the conscious adjustment of therapeutic reinforcers to differences in client values makes behavior therapy universally applicable, precluding problems of cultural or class bias in treatment.[6] But if the behavioral approach is as effective, efficient and universal as its proponents claim, it is even more important that social workers consider the broader political and/or organizational consequences of its practice.

Theory versus practice

The term 'therapeutic technology' is used here to refer to the means and ends of therapy. It focuses on what therapists do *in practice* rather than on what they might do *in theory*. All therapeutic technologies are inherently political. First, they contain within them tacit theories of social problems and social change. Second, they imply political decisions about problem definitions and targets of intervention. Third, they prescribe and proscribe what are ultimately political roles for the therapist, the client, and representatives of the larger society. Fourth, they allocate different degrees of power to each of these groups for decision-making within the therapeutic context. Finally, the implementation of a therapeutic technology has consequences for the future political attitudes and actions of those who are treated.

The politics of problem definitions

The political character of a therapeutic technology is nowhere better revealed than in an examination of the ways in which client problems are defined. On this point, Cloward and Epstein comment:[7]

> It is characteristic of human societies that social problems of various kinds are defined as resulting, not from institutional inadequacies, but from the presumed moral, social, or psychological defects of the people implicated in those problems. To the extent that these definitions are successfully imposed, criticism is deflected from the social order and support is mobilized for the maintenance of the existing system of social arrangements. Hence such definitions are essentially conservative; they tend to preserve the institutional *status quo*.

The foregoing statement was written to describe the conservative bias in psychoanalytic casework. In theory the behavioral approach avoids this bias. Behaviorists have publicly rejected the 'disease model' implicit in the psychiatric approach. Thus, Thomas suggests that behavior therapists do not view behavior as 'inherently psychopathological, deviant or maladaptive.' He adds that for the behaviorist 'behavior is behavior.'[8]

Observation of behavioral practice and a reading of practice papers however reveals an ominously familiar pattern. For while behavioral theory rejects invidious labels for client behavior, practitioners almost universally view their task as the identification and reduction of 'problematic,' 'deviant' or 'maladaptive' *client* behavior. In other words the client remains culpable. He is no longer sick. Now he is viewed as someone who 'does not adequately perform social roles.'[9] Alternatively, he is someone who has not learned to 'manage' his own behavior.[10] And the legitimacy of institutionally defined roles and definitions of deviance remains unquestioned.

So, for example, in a recent article, the USA's foremost behaviorist B. F. Skinner views the alienation of youth in American society purely in terms of the behaviors of young people which are obnoxious to their elders. He says:[11]

> Consider the fact that increasingly large numbers of young
> people are behaving in ways that deeply disturb their elders.
> Young people stay aloof from their families or leave home
> altogether. They neglect the social amenities; they are poorly
> dressed, dirty and rude. They take time off from school or
> from the university or drop out completely. They work, if at all,
> irregularly and indifferently, and many are content to beg for
> the things they need. They steal and condone stealing, calling
> the police 'pigs' and attack them for enforcing the law. They
> desecrate flags, burn draft-cards, refuse to serve in the armed
> forces. . . .

It does not immediately follow from this account of youthful alienation that the 'problem' is with the young. One might just as easily question prevailing forms of the family as an institution, institutionally defined dress and conduct codes, the character and relevance of the educational system, the nature of modern capitalism, the arbitrary exercise of authority by the police, and the continuation of the war in Vietnam as the 'problem.' Skinner does not. He simply concludes that young people's 'values are wrong'.

In fairness to Skinner it should be pointed out that he suggests that the solution to the problem of youthful alienation involves changing institutions so that they are just and equitable in their allocation of rewards and punishments. He is silent, however, about how to bring about such reforms.

In practice, behavioral programs for social reform are more likely to be repressive devices of social control. One example is a recently publicized behavioral welfare program that has been proposed for experimental use in New York State. This program would cut sharply family benefits to a level far below minimal need and award money for such activities as mothers and children tracking down deserting fathers, mothers establishing the paternity of illegitimate children, etc. In the behavioral jargon of its designers, this is an 'incentive for independence program'. However, the Columbia University Center for Social Policy and Law terms it 'a primitive form of coercion.'[12]

Some behavioral programs not only imply client culpability but explicitly reinforce it. The Essexfield delinquency project, for example, provided systematic rewards for delinquents 'telling their stories' about why they became delinquent in terms of 'more conventional definitions of their own deviance and the factors that led to the deviancy in the first place.' This was necessary in order that the boys might 'properly assume the role of the "helped person." '[13]

Descriptions of individual treatment cases as well support the generalization that behavior therapists derive their treatment goals from the most conventional and conservative definitions of appropriate social behavior, even when these definitions are challenged by large segments of the society. Stuart, for example, discusses his treatment of a twenty-one-year-old woman who is suffering from chronic anxiety after having undergone her second abortion. He describes the client's situation as follows:[14]

> Alice's life was characterized by instability at the time
> treatment began. She had changed her job eight times in the
> previous two years and was then employed as an office 'girl
> friday' at a very low salary. She had many boyfriends ...
> during the same two years. Alice was an extremely attractive
> young woman who had no difficulty in meeting men, although
> she had great difficulty in maintaining a relationship with men.
> She would meet a man who interested her, would become
> sexually involved immediately, and would develop an intense
> dependency, soon after which she would be abandoned.

In his treatment of this woman, Stuart does not raise questions about the relationship between her problems and the role-definitions which are imposed upon women in American society. Nor does he begin with an analysis of her work experience or the effects of her unwanted pregnancies and the conditions under which they were terminated. Instead, like his Freudian predecessors, and like Alice as well, he becomes 'sexually involved immediately' and sets out to change Alice's dating and ultimately her sexual behavior. In doing so he emphasizes and reinforces conformity to conservative definitions of how 'ladies' are supposed to behave:[15]

> It was suggested that if she create a different aura of expectation
> about herself, her dates would respond differently. Thus, she
> was instructed to wait for her dates to help her on with her
> coat, open doors, light her cigarettes for her, and the like. In
> short, she was instructed on how to *act like a lady so that others
> would treat her like a lady*. [Our italics]

Along similar lines, a behavior-modification training film produced by the Hartwig Project—an anti-delinquency program in the inner city of Detroit—shows how a Black teenager is trained to say 'Yes, Mrs Jackson' to his teacher whenever he is inclined to be noncompliant. This feat is accomplished by writing the three magic words on a card which is placed in the boy's pocket. The therapist then plays the role of Mrs Jackson and tries to incite the boy to anger. When he feels anger, the boy is instructed to touch the card in his pocket and remember what is written upon it. After a number of role-plays, he is able to say 'Yes, Mrs Jackson' without even touching the card. There is no discussion of the race question, no consideration of the possible inadequacies of the school system or the teacher. The youth is simply told that this technique will help him get along better in school. It is assumed that his former classroom behavior was inappropriate. He is the target of change and the change is always in the direction of compliance.

Of course, more dramatic examples might be offered of the use of aversive conditioning techniques such as electric shock and nausea-inducing drugs to 'treat' homosexuals, exhibitionists, gamblers and other socially defined deviants. But in many respects the less dramatic examples are more important to consider. These are the interventions which go unexamined in the press of daily practice.

The treatment contract

In contrast to the psychiatric approach, most descriptions of behavior therapy stress the 'contractual' relationship between therapist and patient. Sulzer, for example, describes the behavior therapist as an 'agent of the patient, [who] undertakes to treat only what is specifically determined jointly by the patient and therapist.'[16] However, Scheff's work on the 'negotiation of reality' between therapist and patient shows how much more skilled therapists are in making their definitions stick.[17] In that study of a psychoanalytic intake interview, the therapist uses his superior status and negotiating skills systematically to invalidate the problem definitions that the patient brings to the intake interview.

Similarly, a paper written recently by a team of behavioral social workers suggests that in preparation for setting the terms of the treatment contract, the behavioral therapist should 'obtain the client descriptions of presenting problems and, as the interview proceeds, he also lists the *more conspicuous problems he himself discerns*' [Our italics].[18]

The non-contractual nature of the treatment contract is more obvious when the client is someone who has been successfully labeled as deviant or potentially deviant, although the participatory rhetoric persists. In the Hartwig anti-delinquency project mentioned earlier, for example, referrals of the names of 'delinquency-prone' youngsters are taken from the police. The validity of the label is never questioned and an attempt is made 'to take every child into treatment who is referred.'[19] Although participation is defined as voluntary, Rose points out that 'low motivation' clients are often treated to a visit to a local reformatory to 'confront them with the ultimate consequences of their potential deviance.'[20]

In his paper on 'behavioral contracting', Stuart describes a case in which a sixteen-year-old girl was referred to a behaviorally-oriented social-work agency by the juvenile court. The girl's elderly parents had had her committed to a private psychiatric hospital following 'alleged promiscuity, exhibitionism, drug abuse and home truancy,' labels over which there can be considerable disagreement. When they could no longer afford private hospitalization, the parents petitioned the court to assume wardship for the girl. Because the allegations could not stand up in court, the girl was placed back in her parents' home and referred to the behavioral treatment agency. There a 'treatment contract' was set based on voluntary compliance. When the girl refused to comply with the terms of the contract, a new one was set—this one based on a coercive alliance between the girl's parents, the court and the social work agency. Thus, despite the democratic imagery of the contract idea, a court order was secured which proscribed the girl from entering either of the two local communes in which her friends resided. By her 'therapist,' she was 'made to understand that, should she be found in either commune, not she but the commune members would be liable to prosecution for contributing to the delinquency of a minor.'[21]

In closed institutions—prisons, mental hospitals, reformatories—the therapeutic tyranny is complete. Inmates have nothing to say about treatment goals. Here the contract is between the therapist and the organization. And most behaviorists seem untroubled by the exclusion of the client from these decisions. Thomas, for example, observes that to do behavior therapy, 'someone has to define it [behavior] as problematic.' He goes on to say that he sees 'no great problem' with who does the defining.[22]

What I am suggesting is that in treatment situations in which client and therapist agree on problem definitions and treatment goals, there *is* no great problem to it. This pattern is most likely to occur in private practice with middle-class adult clients. But in those situations in which client and therapist disagree, in those situations in which the client is coerced into participation, there is a problem and the problem is resolved politically. It is resolved on the basis of who has the power to impose his definition of the client's reality. In this context the therapist almost always wins. The only alternatives open to the client are mock-compliance or non-compliance. For each of these alternatives however the client is likely to pay a high price and the result is usually further alienation.

The client as uncontrollable child

One way in which the usurpation of the client's contractual rights is justified is by the use of the metaphor of the client as an uncontrollable child; he is infantilized so that his definitions of reality may be invalidated. So, for example, when Thomas discusses treatment situations in which the client's right to define treatment goals are taken away, he cites the case of a child who has temper tantrums. He points out that 'the child didn't say, "I have a problem and I want to be helped," and the child was not consulted concerning his willingness to stop having tantrums.'[23] From this he comfortably extends the image to include all 'those persons whose behavior is initially defined as problematic mainly by others, not by themselves.'

But oppressed people who act in their own interest and who challenge the institutional *status quo* are not children having temper tantrums. They have the ability and the right to define their own problems.

In addition, behavioral theorists operate on the assumption that 'covert mentalistic formulations,'[24] i.e. understanding of one's situation, is irrelevant to therapy. Thus, in contrast to the psychoanalytic approach which treated the low-income client as though he had false consciousness (thinking his problems were environmental when they were really psychological), the behaviorists prefer to treat their clients as though they were and should be unconscious. The consequence is the same however. Clients are systematically deflected from seeing their socio-political position in society. In short, behavioral practice puts theory to work for the power structure—molding, shaping and shocking people into roles which people in power define as preferable.

The place of environmental manipulation

Another consequence of the emphasis on client culpability is a continuation of the earlier de-emphasis on environmental manipulation in the client's behalf. Here again the distinction between theory and practice is critical. In theory, the behavior therapist is as much involved in altering the 'controlling conditions' which perpetuate the client's problem as he is with changing the client. In practice, however, behavior therapists seem as unwilling to challenge existing institutional arrangements as their psychoanalytic predecessors. For Stuart, environmental manipulation means convincing a suicidal secretary to change her job.[25]

More commonly, environmental manipulation is seen as persuading others in the client's environment to use behavioral techniques to modify the client's behavior.[26] For the most part, however, the client's environment is treated as static, unchangeable and above all, legitimate.

Organizational application of behavioral techniques

What happens when behavioral techniques are introduced into organizations? One frequent outcome is the familiar process of goal-displacement—where therapeutic means are displaced from therapeutic ends. Rather, they become techniques for making the organization run smoother. So, for example, in mental hospitals, token economies are frequently used to get patients to do unpleasant tasks such as ward cleaning and washing other patients. Thomas suggests that *in principle* there is no reason why token economies cannot be applied to behavior that 'more obviously relates to therapeutic objectives.'[27] But are they?

Elsewhere, Thomas cites a case study in which behavioral techniques were actually used by psychiatric nurses on a mental patient.[28]

> Consider the case of Lucille, a patient in a mental hospital who had been making frequent visits to the nurses' office for a period of two years. During the *pretreatment* study it was found that she entered the nurses' office an average of sixteen times a day. The nurses had resigned themselves to this activity on the grounds that such efforts as pushing her back bodily onto the ward had failed in the past and because the patient had been classified as mentally defective and therefore 'too dumb' to understand. [Our italics.]

The 'treatment' regimen prescribed for Lucille involved instructing the nurses systematically to ignore Lucille's efforts to receive attention. In a very short time, the behaviors which staff found obnoxious were effectively 'extinguished.' 'Treatment' was then 'terminated.' Apparently, Lucille wasn't so dumb after all. Thomas doesn't tell us what happened to Lucille.

In the field of education, 'classroom management techniques' (a remarkably appropriate term) are likely to be used for control rather than educational ends. A review of the literature in this field indicates that frequently the measure of success of a program of intervention is the increase in such behaviors as sitting quietly in one's seat, raising one's hand before speaking, facing forward, etc.[29]

The connection between these behaviors and educational ends is simply assumed.

In organizations in which a range of professional specialities are present, behavioral programs may become an arena in which inter-professional rivalries are played out—at the client's expense. Thomas describes a token economy system in a mental hospital where patients had to earn the right to interviews with social workers, psychologists and other staff.[30] He happily points out that patients needed 20 tokens to see a ward psychologist and 100 to see a social worker. Incidentally, he says, the latter was the most expensive of all. One can guess who set the prices.

In social work, it is often argued that commitment to professional norms will prevent abuses of this technology. Recent empirical research on the role-orientation of social workers however indicates that social workers see their primary commitment to the norms of the agencies in which they work.[31] The consequence, one would predict, will be the use of behavioral techniques for organizational ends.

The tendency toward goal-displacement is heightened by the teaching of behavioral techniques to lower-level staff in prisons, mental hospitals, etc. Thus, prison guards and mental-hospital ward attendants—neither of whom are noted for their therapeutic sensibilities—are now being instructed in behavioral methods. How they will employ these powerful techniques is an open question. Or is it?

Summary and conclusions

In this paper I have set forth the preposition that behavior therapy, in practice, is as conservative and élitist a therapeutic technology as was the early psychiatric approach to casework. This is evident in: (1) the continuing emphasis on client culpability in problem definitions; (2) the non-contractual nature of the treatment contract; (3) the imagery of the client as an uncontrollable child; and (4) the continuing de-emphasis on environmental manipulation on the client's behalf. Finally, I described the pervasive tendency toward displacement of therapeutic goals in organizations that employ behavioral techniques.

To conclude I would agree with the behaviorists that social casework needs a new model of practice. But what is needed is a model of radical casework.[32] Such an approach would be oriented to social change rather than to social control. It would begin with the assumption that the client knows what is in his best interest. This is what some social work scholars have called advocacy.[33] By advocacy I mean a technology for caseworkers which begins with

the client's definition of his problem and places the client's definition in a political context. It is a model which links the client's
individual interest with his collective interests. It is a model which
makes use of the social worker's knowledge, status and willingness
to engage in conflict in the client's behalf. It is a model which
explores the mental health potentials of social action activities, i.e.
of clients acting in their own behalf. As Bond put it:[34]

> This sort of casework would involve the worker in developing
> techniques of raising the client's level of consciousness about
> his deprivations; in making the client angry rather than cooling
> him out; in linking up angry clients with common problems so
> that they can exploit their collective power; and even in
> becoming angry enough himself to become an advocate for his
> client's rights against all opposition.

In contrast to this approach, much of contemporary casework
reflects what Philip Slater in his insightful book, *The Pursuit of
Loneliness*, referred to as the 'toilet assumption.' In his chapter
entitled, 'I Only Work Here,' Slater says:[35]

> Our ideas about institutionalizing the aged, psychotic, retarded
> and infirm are based on a pattern of thought that we might call
> the Toilet Assumption—the notion that unwanted matter,
> unwanted difficulties, unwanted complexities and obstacles will
> disappear if they are removed from out immediate field of
> vision. We do not connect the trash we throw from the car
> window with the trash in our streets, and we assume that
> replacing old buildings with new expensive ones will alleviate
> poverty and slums. We throw the aged and psychotic into
> institutional holes where they cannot be seen. Our approach to
> social problems is to decrease their visibility; out of sight out of
> mind. This is the real foundation of racial segregation,
> especially its most extreme case, the Indian 'Reservation.' The
> result of our social efforts has been to remove the underlying
> problems of our society farther and farther from daily experience
> and daily consciousness, and hence to decrease, in the mass of
> the population, the knowledge, skill, resources, and motivation
> necessary to deal with them.
> When these discarded problems rise to the surface again—
> a riot, a protest, an expose in the mass media—we react as
> if a sewer had backed up. We are shocked, disgusted, and
> angered, and immediately call for the emergency plumber (the
> special commission, the crash program) to ensure that the
> problem is once again removed from consciousness.

What I am suggesting here is that behavior therapy is the new way in which social workers can do society's dirty work—all the time telling themselves, their clients, and the rest of society that the work is not only hygienic but professional as well.

Notes

1 Richard A. Cloward and Irwin Epstein, 'Private social welfare's disengagement from the poor: the case of family adjustment agencies,' in George A. Brager and Francis P. Purcell (eds), *Community Action Against Poverty*, College and University Press, New Haven, 1967, pp. 40-63.

2 Paul L. Adams and Nancy F. McDonald, 'Clinical cooling out of poor people,' *American Journal of Orthopsychiatry*, 38 : 3 (April 1968), pp. 457-63.

3 Edwin J. Thomas, 'Selected sociobehavioral techniques and principles: an approach to interpersonal helping,' *Social Work*, 13 : 1 (January 1968), pp. 25-6.

4 For the seminal article on the political implications of functional and diagnostic social casework, see Alan Keith-Lucas, 'The political theory implicit in social casework theory, *American Political Science Review*, 57 : 4 (December 1953), pp. 1076-91.

5 It should be pointed out that the material for this paper was selected on the basis of the degree to which it generated questions for further inquiry. The review is in no way meant to be representative of the behavioral literature as a whole.

6 Glenn Terrell, Jr, Kathryn Durkin, and Melvin Wiesley, 'Social class and the nature of the incentive in discrimination learning,' *Journal of Abnormal and Social Psychology*, 59 : 2 (September 1959), pp. 270-72.

7 Cloward and Epstein, op. cit., p. 57.

8 Edwin J. Thomas, 'The socio-behavioral approach: illustrations and analysis,' in Edwin J. Thomas (ed.), *The Socio-Behavioral Approach and Applications to Social Work*, Council on Social Work Education, New York, 1967, pp. 11, 16.

9 Rosemary C. Sarri and Robert D. Vinter, 'Organizational requisites for a socio-behavioral technology, in Thomas (ed.), op. cit., p. 88.

10 Eileen D. Gambrill, Edwin J. Thomas, and Robert D. Carter, 'Procedure for socio-behavioral practice in open settings,' *Social Work*, 16 : 1 (January 1971), p. 61.

11 B. F. Skinner, 'B. F. Skinner says what's wrong with the social sciences,' *Listener*, 86 : 2218 (September 1971), p. 430.

12 Nick Kotz, 'Earning your dole,' *Washington Post*, 11 October 1971.

13 Thomas, op. cit., p. 5.

14 Richard B. Stuart, 'Analysis and illustration of the process of assertive conditioning,' paper presented at the 16th Annual Forum of the National Conference of Social Welfare, Dallas (24 May 1967), p. 4.

15 Ibid., p. 13.

16 Edward S. Sulzer, 'Research frontier: reinforcement and the therapeutic contract,' *Journal of Counseling Psychology*, 9 : 3 (Fall 1962), p. 271.

17 Thomas J. Scheff, 'Negotiating reality: notes on power in the assessment of responsibility,' *Social Problems*, 16 : 1 (Summer 1968), pp. 3-17.

18 Gambrill, *et al.*, op. cit., p. 52.

19 Sheldon D. Rose, 'Discussion,' in Thomas (ed.), op. cit., p. 56.

20 Ibid., p. 58.

21 Richard B. Stuart, 'Behavioral contracting within the families of delinquents,' *Journal of Behavior Therapy and Experimental Psychiatry*,

2:1 (March 1971), pp. 1-11.
22 Edwin J. Thomas, 'Discussion,' in Thomas (ed.), op. cit., p. 37.
23 Ibid., p. 58.
24 Stuart, in Thomas (ed.), op. cit., p. 23.
25 Ibid., pp. 37-8.
26 Gambrill *et al.*, op. cit., p. 55.
27 Thomas, in Thomas (ed.), op. cit., p. 7.
28 Thomas, 'Selected socio-behavioral techniques ...,' *Social Work*, 13:1 (January 1968), p. 19.
29 Donald L. Macmillan and Steven R. Forness, 'Behavior modification: limitations and liabilities,' *Exceptional Children*, (December 1970), pp. 291-7.
30 Thomas, in Thomas (ed.), op. cit., p. 6.
31 Irwin Epstein, 'Professionalization, professionalism and social-worker radicalism,' *Journal of Health and Social Behavior*, 11:1 (March 1970), pp. 67-77.
32 For an articulation of this model of practice, see Martin Rein, 'Social work in search of a radical profession,' *Social Work*, 15:2 (April 1970), pp. 13-28.
33 See, for example, Richard A. Cloward and Richard M. Elman, 'Advocacy in the ghetto,' *Transaction*, 4:2 (December 1966), pp. 27-35.
34 Nick Bond, 'The case for radical casework,' *Social Work Today*, 2:9 (July 1971), p. 23.
35 Philip Slater, *The Pursuit of Loneliness*, Beacon Press, Boston, 1970, p. 15.

10

Making use of research
Ian Shaw

Introduction

This paper examines some criticisms made by social workers about research. It argues that this criticism is valid on a number of counts, but that overstatement and misunderstanding of the assumptions made by researchers seriously weaken its main thrust. Published research, correctly evaluated and applied, is a relatively untapped resource for social work practice, policy-making and administration. Maximum utilisation of research material depends on a realistic recognition of difficulties. Some researchers have erred in assuming that utilisation is a simple matter, whereas social workers have tended to fall into the opposite trap of thinking it is impossible.

Attitudes to research

Notwithstanding the increasing amount of published research on social work, frequent complaints are heard that social workers do not read research and are not influenced by it; that agencies make little attempt to make sense of their own statistics; that questions of 'basic' research interest are sidestepped; and that the schools of social work, social work agencies and the professional associations have made comparatively few major research contributions. [1, 2, 3] On the other hand, it is difficult to see how social workers can improve their practice so that it meets human needs more closely without some form of evaluation through research.

Social workers manifest for example, an attitude of 'practical scepticism' towards theoretical knowledge. Adhering strongly to a belief in the uniqueness of the individual, they are reluctant to entertain generalisations. General rules are held to be restrictive, and the objectivity of science is seen as inferior to the warmth and spontaneity of the social worker's relationship with his client.

Because the social worker is dealing with the whole of the human condition at any one time, he feels he cannot isolate and objectify.

A belief that the true value of man is not fully comprehended in his day-to-day behaviour—an assumption expressed in the notion of acceptance—leads the social worker to resist any approach which appears to group people on the basis of shared, outward characteristics. Elizabeth Irvine gives expression to this when she writes that 'science deals splendidly with all that can be weighed, measured or counted, but this involves excluding from the universe of discourse the intangible, the imponderable, all that cannot be reduced to statistics'.[4]

Confronted by this attitude, the more 'tough minded' social worker has often appeared to be at a loss. The welfare professions, it is argued, should set themselves precise goals, capable of achievement; they ought to recognise that their cases possess common factors, and act on that knowledge.[5] But welfare practitioners rarely establish specific and limited objectives. Indeed, the activities of social workers often seem to be ends in themselves. This explains why it is sometimes difficult to detect whether social workers are discussing values or techniques when they talk about client self-determination, etc. The idea of social work as a vocation, still strongly held, leads social workers to resist notions of efficiency. Work is justified in terms of ideals, and not in terms of any known degree of efficiency in the pursuit of a given goal, and social workers rarely observe the conceptual distinction between ideals and objective success. Therefore, when practitioners speak of having aims, the reference is not to planning feasible social provision, but to the personal ethics of the practitioner. For example, there is sometimes a reluctance to face up to limitations of resources available to an agency, stemming from an ideal of never withholding help.[6]

The argument that sees the welfare professions as strongly vocational in character, pursuing aims cast in the form of ideals to be striven towards, rather than guides to action in particular situations leads to criticism of particular research studies, some of which is justified. For example, some research studies, in their quest for objectivity, end by adopting inappropriate criteria of success and failure.

For instance, the research project, 'Girls at Vocational High'[7] examined a group of 189 girls assessed as 'potential problem cases' who were referred to the Youth Consultation Service in New York. These girls were contrasted with a control group of 192 girls, who were similarly assessed on entry to high school. At the close of the project, the authors could detect no appreciable differences between the girls who had received social work help and those who had been allocated to the 'no treatment' group. However, as an assessment of outcome this research is open to the serious criticism that the criteria used by the researchers such as out-of-wedlock pregnancies and truancy, were quite irrelevant to the treatment goals actually pursued within the agency, with their emphasis on increasing self-understanding.

Attempts to measure the outcome of social work are criticised further for making assumptions (e.g. in studies which rest on the use of control groups) that present a picture of social work methods that over-simplifies the complex personal interactions involved. For example, in the project 'Helping the Aged'[9] an attempt was made to assess whether the elderly clients of a welfare department in a London borough were helped more effectively by trained social workers than by untrained workers. The old people were allocated on a random basis between the two forms of treatment. Assessments were made by a social worker and medical practitioner at the time of allocation and again at the end of the project, in order to measure changes taking place in the life and situation of the old people during the experiment. The assumption is made that the differences in treatment styles between social workers can be clearly identified. Unfortunately it is as yet not possible to say that we 'know' the constituent elements of social work treatment in the same sense that we 'know', for example, the ingredients of drugs tested in medical trials. Moreover, even if this assumption is granted, how can we be sure that the treatments given to the old people in the experimental and control groups are representative of any wider categories of treatments offered by social workers at other times and in other situations? And if we cannot do this, we cannot generalise from the experiment.

Practitioners have also been quick to enter reservations on ethical grounds against experimental trials in social work in which a group given a treatment measure is compared with a group from whom the treatment is withheld. Social work resources are scarce, and practitioners are unlikely to smile on experimental projects which necessitate denying help to a group of clients manifesting a particular need. In the study of elderly people referred to above, this was overcome by comparing two different forms of treatment, rather than contrasting a group receiving treatment with a second group receiving no help at all. Social workers are especially critical, where allocation to the two groups is made on a random basis. This is illustrated by a recent controlled trial of a 'therapeutic community' in an approved school, in which, because of opposition by practitioners to the notion of the 'therapeutic community', the number of boys allocated to the training school by the regional classifying school began to fall from about the time random allocation was introduced, and rose rapidly after the close of the experiment.[8]

In recent years a number of atheoretical studies, in which situations have been seen through the client's eyes, have appeared, [9], [10], [11], [12] and this can be seen in part as a reaction against atomistic and 'objective' analyses of particular personal and character traits, which ignore the complexity of the personality. Irrespective of whether such an approach will be vindicated by results, it represents a further concession to criticisms by social work practitioners.

It is the same attitude which leads social workers to argue that the only worthwhile kind of knowledge is that based on their personal experience. Research findings on the other hand are criticised as 'simply common sense', while at the same time a marked reluctance is manifested to entertain research which contradicts common sense. Thus the response to research findings tends to be either 'I do not believe it', or else 'I knew it already'. This stems from an attitude which views social work as a comparatively simple activity in danger of mystification by researchers. 'Theory' and 'practice' are separated, as are 'thought' and 'feeling', and in each case the social worker is prone to submit the former to the latter. 'Doing is finally wrenched apart from describing, and no-one apparently recognises the importance of the question, How do I know when I get it right?'[13]

The practitioners' wariness of generalisation is often viewed by them as essentially a moral position, which can be stated with difficulty, and argued not at all. The controversy here is often about the moral status of 'means'. For example, the claim is sometimes made that the welfare professions now possess a number of authentic 'techniques'—ECT, drugs, behaviour therapy, etc. Arguments by practitioners for the rejection of these techniques often run on the lines that they are not effective 'in the long run'. This argument hides what appears to be the real basis of practitioners' objections, which is that to treat people in such a way is to deal with them improperly. In particular, techniques are felt to be permissible only if they deal with people at the level of conscious choice. There is a difference between 'effectiveness' and 'justifiability'; a fact which such arguments often seem not to acknowledge. But in any case to apply science to human subjects does not necessarily involve regarding them in a non-moral fashion. In medicine, for instance, an ethical code governing clinical and nonclinical research has been drawn up,[14] explicitly based on the assumption that a human subject on whom experiments may be carried out is a person with rights and powers of choice. Social work researchers can and sometimes do take the same view. Social workers might concentrate on pressing for this rather than on a blanket condemnation of research as such.[15]

A further complaint that researchers, in generalising, deny the individuality of the client, betrays a failure adequately to understand the character of much of their own social work activity. In coming to grips with a particular situation involving the client, the social worker does in practice engage in generalisation. The individual occupying a role as client is approached as a representative of a particular type, to whom lessons learned about previous examples of the type may properly be applied. In other words, a generalisation is being made from a series of specific instances—an unacknowledged and statistically unanalysed sampling procedure. Even the simplest so-called practical task is rooted in a set of underlying general assumptions through which it is structured and defined. Many of the 'taken for granted' tasks of social work with children, for example, are based on assumptions about the importance of the family and parent-child relationships. In rejecting 'evidence' in favour of 'experience', the social worker is embarking on (inefficient) probability theory thinking. The sample upon which he bases his conclusions is likely to be unrepresentative as to clients, records and social work practice.*

Thus the weaknesses of outcome studies, the oversimplified assumptions made in the use of control groups, the ethical reservations held against experimental trials and the need to do justice to the complexity of the human personality, are each tenable criticisms of some research in the welfare professions. But social workers have failed to see that in admitting the claims of research they do not have to deny the individuality and rights of their clients. [6, 15, 16, 17]

Application of research

There is obviously need for a better mutual understanding between social workers and researchers, and this applies to the application of research as much as to its execution. There are hopeful signs in this direction, specifically in the examining of difficulties encountered in the application of knowledge gained from research to the professional objectives of the social worker or the administrator.

This is very necessary. For example, the impression is that research projects tend to be recalled by practitioners, if at all, by the single, striking finding. While this perpetuates the memory of particular studies, it impoverishes the critical assessment and utilisation of data. But the social worker receives little help in this

* The social worker does have the advantage that his probability thinking is likely to be fairly tentative. Research, if inadequately executed or understood, could produce a more prejudicial form of probability thinking.

respect; many writers on research tend to be indifferent to problems of utilisation.[18] Other writers, although raising the issue, provide little in the way of specific criteria to guide social workers in the task.[19]

So it is not surprising that the latter are somewhat naïve in discussing the benefits to be gained from the social sciences, holding such fallacious beliefs as that social science is put to use simply by popularising its content; or that only research which exactly replicates a practical problem is relevant to it—going on to the claim that the number of social problems with which the practitioner is concerned is so large that a research-based approach is not really practical. This alleged impracticability of research accounts in part for the low esteem in which surveys suggest social workers hold research writing and courses in research, and the low ranking given to research as a source of help in everyday practice.[20, 21, 22]

The ethical issue referred to above is also a problem affecting research utilisation. If it is assumed that any particular research result can give a clear lead as to what action a social worker should take, it can only be by ignoring the ethical element in such decisions —or in a naïve assumption that what is factually true or operationally convenient is also morally justifiable. The value element cannot be disposed of so easily.[6, 23, 24]

The probation service provides an example. Whereas in the past it has been sufficient for the probation officer to exercise oversight or supervision of offenders, and some have given further justification to their work by adducing various ethical aims, such as that of dealing with offenders in what is considered to be a morally justifiable way, there have been a number of developments in the last five years, which have tended to promote an expectation that the probation officer should produce observable changes in the behaviour of his clients. The public and the judiciary have developed more pragmatic expectations of the service than the latter has had of itself. This is one of the factors behind the emergence of community supervision for some who would previously have gone to prison. In addition, the rationale behind the current Home Office Research Unit project, IMPACT,* is clearly based on the assumption that variations in the 'intensiveness' of social work help will be reflected in differences in the observable outcomes among probation orders and aftercare licences. Finally, there has been a slow but definite retreat from casework in the service; this has been on the grounds of practical utility, the adoption of differential methods of practice being accompanied by efforts to evaluate their relative effectiveness.

* Intensive Matching, Probation and Aftercare Treatment.

It can readily be observed from this survey of questions surrounding the potential utility of research that decisions in social work organisations are unlikely to be made on the grounds of rationality alone. This must be taken into account, as well as the simple alternatives of efficiency and inefficiency.

Utilisation by the practitioner

Most people will agree that research, like marriage, is a good thing. But the social worker who claims empirical research to be of value, is often scarcely more influenced by research than those who judge it to be of little or no value.

The problem is of course partly a result of the general distrust of research discussed above. But one suspects that it is also partly a self-perpetuating one, arising from the fact that social workers are not trained to utilise research data, and that in any case the demands of their day-to-day work give no encouragement to the development of abilities for reading and appraising published research. Moreover, is it possible for social workers to learn how to assess and utilise research, without being taught how to carry it out? Social workers, incorrigibly practical in outlook, have little incentive to do this.

Nevertheless there *is* research of value to the practitioner. A growing corpus of work exists which can help the social worker in his understanding of social problems and situations. A considerable amount is known about the conditions of the elderly, including those who resort to social work agencies;[9, 26] much painstaking work has been undertaken to identify the numbers of handicapped people in Great Britain, to examine what local-authority health and welfare services are being made available to them, and to assess the extent and cause of handicap, the degree of independence achieved by handicapped housewives, their housing conditions, and the effect of handicap and physical impairment on ability to get suitable employment, and on social life and leisure activities.[27, 28] The incidence and difficulties attached to different degrees of mental handicap have also been studied,[29, 30, 31] and sustained attempts have been made to gather and interpret facts about the services provided for children. [32, 33] Social workers often seem ignorant of all this and, more importantly, do not know, and receive no guidance, on where to find out what they need.

The social worker might reply at this point that he may be ignorant of the national scene, but he knows his clients. But does he really know what it feels like to be an adoptee, a retarded mother using the social services, an ex-prisoner deciding whether or not to see his aftercare officer, an unmarried mother, a client seeking help with a matrimonial problem, etc.? And would he not benefit by widening his knowledge and so be able to set his clients against the background of a wider sample and a broader context of circumstances. There is also the question of objectivity, which is bound to be affected by his personal involvement with clients. In all such cases research has been carried out which helps the practitioner's understanding. [9, 10, 12, 34, 35]

Research also has much of value to say to the social worker in the developing of skills. A recent writer has argued that: [6]

> The case for group counselling and social casework is not, I think, that they are effective in bringing about demonstrable results, for we have no evidence that they are. The case is that they represent what we at the moment regard as the morally acceptable limits to which we are prepared to go in dealing with people who have not requested our intervention. [6]

Yet the question of what social work achieves in fact remains important and the results of research on this have created a state of chronic tension for social workers during the last few years. We have mounting testimony from research findings that casework if applied indiscriminately to social work clients may be ineffective in achieving demonstrable results. [25] From a number of studies it is sufficient to mention 'Helping the Aged', a project discussed earlier in this paper. [7, 9, 36, 37] A sample of 300 old people, aged seventy or over, and newly referred to the welfare department of a London borough over a ten-month period in 1966, were divided into an experimental and a control group, the former receiving the attention of trained, and the latter of untrained workers.

The findings indicated that in only two factors—the number of practical needs met and the morale level of clients—was the experimental group superior. However, the point is not simply that trained social workers achieved only slightly better results than untrained workers. The experimental group had other advantages as well as any bestowed by training. For example, of the clients seen by untrained social workers, 63 per cent were supervised by more than one worker during the fieldwork, whereas the experimental group enjoyed whatever benefits continuity of attention might afford. Further, the untrained social workers carried a far higher caseload than their trained colleagues, and hence had significantly less time to devote to the needs of their clients. And again, the trained staff had the opportunity of regular case supervision with the director of the project—herself a highly experienced social worker. The untrained workers had to make do with whatever supervision was normally offered in the agency. Finally, it appears that the untrained workers were unaware of the limited period covered by the project. One can speculate that this might make a difference to the degree of motivation and goal-directed activity of the social workers in each group. And yet, with all the advantages of training, continuity of treatment, low caseloads, skilled supervision and greater motivation to do well, the project workers were more effective to only a relatively small degree in helping their elderly clients, as compared with their untrained fellow workers. Findings of this nature, whatever the practitioner's attitude to research, cannot be ignored.

It may however be more helpful to think of the effectiveness of social work in terms of the question: 'What kind of treatment is effective for which kind of client when given by which type of social worker?' Research carried out under the auspices of the California Youth Authority and the Board of Correction has developed this 'horses for courses' approach since the Grants, in 1952, identified a specific relationship between the maturity levels of naval prisoners and the relative degree of success attaching to different kinds of retraining programmes.[38, 39] A number of projects have attempted to develop classifications of types of client, to analyse the components of social work treatment, and to identify relevant personal characteristics of social workers, in order to try to interrelate them. Five variables recur in the literature, viz. the maturity level of clients; the size of the supervisor's workload; the statistical risk of relapse or failure in different types of case; a distinction between supervision oriented to the outside world of the client and that directed to his inner world; and the different 'styles' of work found among social workers. The Home Office Research Unit has been heavily influenced by this tradition, as indicated by the 'IMPACT' project. But the indications generally are for discrimination in approaches, rather than for any wholesale flight from casework, perhaps to group work, family therapy or community work. The same questioning must be applied to these areas of the social worker's activity also.

Utilisation by the policy-maker

The distinction between policy-makers and administrators is a somewhat arbitrary one, even within an organisation. Various policy-making levels can be identified ranging from parliamentary legislation, through the intermediate level of bodies like the Home Office, to the committees of individual fieldwork agencies. The safest distinction is to locate broad decisions about objectives, involving value choices with the policy-maker and implementation based on the facts of the case with the administrator. However, since factual judgments will be implied in policy decisions, policy-makers must formulate not merely programmes of action in isolation, but review factual information on the objective con-sequences of the alternatives that are available.* And these facts with strong policy implications will be supplied to them by the full-time administrator. It is all a question of emphasis.

The policy-maker needs to be aware of the difficulties which arise in the application of research, because of the way in which policies are formulated. Policy statements are often intended to serve for an undefined period; the assumptions and objectives of the policy-makers are seldom explicit; and policies are never single-minded, but result from the struggle between competing demands. For example, recent legislation in the penal field continues to support a dual system of sentencing: the tariff system and individualised sentences. This is the result of policy-makers trying to secure different things at the same time.[19, 40, 41]

Despite these complexities, research does have scope as an aid to social policy and reform. First, it plays an important part in ascertaining the scale and character of social problems. For example, the concept of 'social need', although not new, has become more important recently particularly since the publication of the Seebohm Report. There have been some useful recent dis-cussions of this concept, bringing out the variety of meanings which can be attached to the idea.[41] The Seebohm Report, although basing its argument for a unified approach to social service provision on this concept by focusing on family and community breakdown, is not clear on how needs are to be detected and measured. Among the meanings used by the committee were administrative categories of need (such as official scales of assistance); concepts like preven-tion, which are used in social work thinking; the clients' own perception of need, as measured by criteria like waiting lists for different kinds of residential care for the mentally ill, the handi-capped or the elderly; a community consensus on what counts as need, as seen in the shared belief that handicapped people living at home require a greater variety of forms of help than a similar person accommodated residentially; and finally, expert diagnosis on what is needed, such as an extension of domiciliary services.[43, 48] A research-oriented approach necessitates some clarification of this key concept.

Reference has been made in the previous section to a number of existing studies which have been addressed to defining social problems, measuring their extent and identifying their causes, to

* Conversely, since value choices are always also being made by admini-strators, they must be responsive to community values.

which can be added the work done by the Child Poverty Action Group. These studies indicated how research can be an instrument of social reform when deliberately applied to social policy issues, and in forming the social climate in which policy choices are made.

Research can go further than this by analysing particular policy proposals, and evaluating their consequences when translated into action. For example, the Seebohm Report makes use of a number of assumptions to account for shortcomings in existing services. Poor client access to services is regarded as a consequence of the division of responsibility for the client; poor co-ordination is a function of lack of resources and divided responsibilities; inadequate provision and the poor adaptability of services are both assumed to be the result of inadequate knowledge or lack of resources. In summary, the report conveys the picture that shortcomings of the social services arise from the then existing organisational structure, whether through insufficient resources, inadequate knowledge or divided responsibilities.[43] The significant point is that few, if any, of these assumptions have been researched to find out what truth, if any, they contain.

Perhaps in recognition of such criticisms, the 1972 Criminal Justice Act has provided for organised feedback of the results of the innovations in social policy made in the Act.[41] Research has been linked to the day training centres and to community service orders. The Home Office Research Unit has been expanded, and the political decisions made at the end of the experimental phase will be influenced by the results of evaluative research. The 1972 Act itself can be seen in part as reflecting the influence of the rather negative results of the research on casework probation in the 1960s. The day centres, for example, are aimed at influencing the client's life on a much broader front than that provided by traditional casework methods.

This is not to say that all or even many policy problems can be overcome with the aid of research. Events are always liable to overtake research, and there are difficulties attached to obtaining definitive answers. And the research result rarely matches exactly to the decision that has to be taken. The policy-maker is still called upon to exercise judgment when adopting policies. Furthermore, the need for politically attractive solutions, rather than scientifically sound research, can undermine the most admirable of research-guided policy solutions.[44]

Utilisation by the administrator

The social work administrator (usually a senior officer in a social work agency) is concerned with efficiency, standards of public service, job satisfaction and many other conceptions. On the one hand, he cannot afford to be utopian about such ideas by displaying indifference to the hard facts of practice. On the other hand, he may wish to avoid the cynicism of using ideas emotively, for persuasive purposes, while privately regarding them as vacuous. In other words, the administrator is faced with trying to bridge the gulf between the unanalysed abstractions which ideals are, and the real life in which actual decisions must be taken. As the role of research in social work agencies can be defined in almost identical terms, the connection between administration and research activity scarcely needs stating.

It should be noticed that this presupposes a difference between research conducted in the universities and research in public service departments. The latter will find difficulty in securing acceptance in the agency, except on the grounds that it yields information of value to management.[45] The implications of this are not always appreciated by research staff in local authorities. Their objection to being confined sometimes to supplying information is based on a misapprehension. Management *needs* well-organised information, accompanied by explanation and interpretation. Moreover the researcher does then share in the making of agency policy, by providing such data as a basis for projecting the future supply of and demand for resources. Senior agency administrators, though ostensibly subordinate in policy matters to lay committees, do lead the latter's thinking in the context of this kind of information. This is not the same as forecasting what is going to happen, but is intended to illuminate the meaning of current trends by showing what will happen if they continue—without implying that they will not change. This includes the difficult task of measuring work and efficiency in the social services.

In assessing supply of and demand for resources, agencies have been perhaps too ready to embark on *ad hoc* surveys to discover unmet needs that the organisation is in no position to meet. The response of some local authorities to the Chronically Sick and Disabled Persons Act has been of this kind. Agencies have repeatedly failed to make use of available material, or to make proper sense of the statistics they already collect. However, if such research shows how far behind needs provision really is, it has its value in spurring on agencies and the public. Reference has for instance already been made to the usefulness of a number of studies in revealing the prevalence of social problems on a national scale. But how many social work agencies have tried to collate from already existing official sources facts about the district for which they provide services, or for their existing and potential clients?[5, 46, 47]

The evaluation of new and existing programmes is the other main function of research in social agencies. Tests of efficiency (however defined) are, of course, an indispensable aid to management in any organisation. The Seebohm Report said nothing new therefore in proclaiming that 'social planning is an illusion without adequate facts; and the adequacy of services mere speculation without evaluation'.[48] In somewhat less epigrammatic language, the same point was made by D. V. Glass as long ago as 1950:[19]

> Given a new service it is surely necessary to include as an
> integral part of the structure some provision for
> examining the results, and for ascertaining how far, and as a
> consequence of which specific measures, the desired ends
> are being achieved. Such provision is far from customary.

Within the Seebohm Report itself can be found a number of claims which can and ought to be evaluated within the local agency. Has the setting up of the new social services department led to growth in the amount of public expenditure on the personal social services? Is the department attracting more trained staff? Does the department respond more quickly to social change? Has a reduction in conflict occurred between the social services and other local authority bodies, and between social workers and members of other professions? Is the department being used by a wider cross-section of the public? What changes have taken place in the role of volunteers and voluntary organisations? Only by detailed local study of these questions can the operation of the new department be justified.

Within his department the administrator is certain to encounter some problems, arising from relations between research staff and practitioners. For example, the social worker might find it difficult in individual cases to maintain a prior agreement with the researcher that respondents (clients) should be expected to participate in an investigation. A similar problem may occur over the question of protecting the confidentiality of the client's disclosures. Also, because social workers assign a higher priority to service than to science, they are likely to press the administrator to allow them to read the report, and will complain if they feel it to be written in pseudo-scientific language not readily turned into practical prescriptions.

The way forward

A number of developments in recent years deserve notice for the contribution they have made to more effective research utilisation. The National Children's Bureau, since its foundation in the 1960s, has undertaken a substantial publication programme, in abstracting research from the child care field. A general abstracting service has been provided by the National Association of Social Workers since 1965, and the *British Journal of Social Work* has recently commenced abstracting articles in the much wider area covered by sociology, psychiatry and psychology, public and social policy and social work, but not including all relevant research. Also, a clearing house has been established at Birmingham University for research carried out in the social service departments.

Further progress seems required in a number of directions:

1 The establishment of an abstracting service is necessary, covering all relevant research, whether conducted in universities or public services.

2 A register should be compiled of research-funding opportunities.

3 A central research register should be kept, perhaps by a body like the Social Science Research Council, of completed and ongoing research in local authorities and universities.

4 Co-operation between local authorities might make some larger-scale and more worthwhile projects possible, and contact with universities give agencies access to resources and expertise not otherwise available.

5 Research feedback is too slow. For some government research a four- or five-year gap between completion of fieldwork and publication is usual, by which time the issue is dead or dying.

6 Social workers should be encouraged, where appropriate, to use measures worked out in research projects for their own practice. For example, the measures of 'personal incapacity' and 'household incapacity' (i.e. the capabilities displayed by the elderly within the home) developed by Peter Townsend, or the measures of mental confusion and depression used in 'Helping the Aged'.[9, 49]

Notes

1 J. W. McCullough, M. J. Brown, and M. Anderson 'A national social work interdisciplinary study of reading behaviour and helpful factors in professional practice', Unpublished, University of Bradford.

2 J. W. McCullough and M. J. Brown, 'Social work educators and social work research', in *Developing Patterns in Social Work Education*, Association of Social Work Teachers, 1970.

3 R. Holman, *Research and Social Work*, BASW Monograph, no. 4, 1970.

4 E. Irvine, 'Education for social work : science or humanity', *Social Work*, 26· 4, 1969.

5 R. J. W. Foren and M. J. Brown, *Planning for Service*, C. Knight, 1971.

6 P. Nokes, *The Professional Task in Welfare Practice*, Routledge & Kegan Paul, 1967.

7 H. J. Meyer, E. F. Borgatta and W. C. Jones, *Girls at Vocational High*, Russell Sage, 1965.

8 R. V. G. Clarke and J. B. Cornish, *The Controlled Trial in Institutional Research*, HMSO, 1972.

9 E. M. Goldberg, *Helping the Aged*, Allen & Unwin, 1970.

10 J. Triseliotis, *In Search of Origins*, Routledge & Kegan Paul, 1973.

11 N. Timms (ed.), *The Receiving End*, Routledge & Kegan Paul, 1973.

12 D. Marsden, *Mothers Alone*, Penguin, 1973.

13 N. Timms, *Language of Social Casework*, Routledge & Kegan Paul, 1968.

14 'Declaration of Helsinki', *British Medical Journal*, 18 July, 1964.

15 D. Emmet, *Rules, Roles and Relations*, Macmillan 1966.

16 G. Smith, 'Everyday theory in social work practice', *Social Work Today*, 2· 3, 1971.

17 S. Briar and H. Miller, *Problems and Issues in Social Casework*, Columbia University Press, 1971.

18 E. Greenwood, 'Social work : a decade of appraisal', *Social Service Review*, 31, 1957.

19 D. V. Glass, 'The application of social research' *British Journal of Sociology*, 1· 1, 1950.

20 T. Tripodi, P. Fellin and H. J. Meyer, *Assessment of Social Research*, F. E. Peacock, 1969.

21 M. J. Brown and J. W. McCullough, 'Reading habits of probation officers', *Probation*, 15· 1, 1969.

22 A. Rosenblatt, 'The practitioner's use and evaluation of research', *Social Work* (USA), 1968.

23 W. Reid and L. Epstein, *Task Oriented Casework*, Columbia University Press, 1972.

24 M. Davies, 'The objectives of the probation service', *British Journal of Social Work*, 2· 4, 1972.

25 J. Fischer, 'Does casework work?' *Social Work*, 18· 1, 1973.

26 E. Shanas, P. Townsend, D. Wedderburn, H. Friis, P. Milhoj, J. Stehouwer, *Old People in Three Industrial Societies*, Routledge & Kegan Paul, 1968.

27 A. I. Harris, E. Cox and C. R. W. Smith, *Handicapped and Impaired in Great Britain*, HMSO, 3 vols, 1971.

28 R. Dinnage, *The Handicapped Child : Research Review*, Longman, 2 vols, 1970, 1972.

29 A. Kushlick, 'A community service for the mentally subnormal', *Social Psychiatry*, 1, 1966, pp. 73-82.

30 M. Bone, B. Spain and F. M. Martin, *Plans and Provisions for the Mentally Handicapped*, Allen & Unwin, 1972.

31 M. Bayley, *Mental Handicap and Community Care*, Routledge & Kegan Paul, 1973.

32 J. Packman, *Child Care : Needs and Numbers*, Allen & Unwin, 1968.

33 B. Davies, A. Barton and I. McMillan, *Variations in Children's Services Among British Urban Authorities*, Bell, 1972.

34 A. Cohen, 'The consumer's view : retarded mothers and the social services', *Social Work Today*, 1· 12, 1971.

35 W. McWilliams and M. Davies, 'Communication about aftercare', *British Journal of Social Work*, 1· 4, 1971.

36 G. E. Brown, *The Multi-Problem Dilemma*, Scarecrow Press, 1968.

37 W. Reid and A. W. Shynne, *Brief and Extended Casework*, Columbia University Press, 1969.

38 R. J. W. Foren and R. Bailey, *Authority in Social Casework*, Pergamon, 1968.

39 T. C. Puckett, 'Can social treatment be effective?' *Social Work Today*, 4· 6, 1973.

40 H. A. Simon, *Administrative Behavior*, Free Press, 1965.

41 M. Davies, 'The Criminal Justice Act 1972 as an expression of social policy', *Social Work Today*, 4· 7, 1973.

42 J. Bradshaw, 'The concept of social need', *New Society*, 30 March 1972.

43 G. Smith, 'Some research implications of the Seebohm Report', *British Journal of Sociology*, 22· 3, 1971.

44 J. Platt, 'Survey data and social policy', *British Journal of Sociology*, 23· 1, 1972.

45 B. Benjamin, 'Research strategies in social service departments', *Journal of Social Policy*, 2· 1, 1973, pp. 13-26.

46 B. Deacon and C. Cannan, 'Social priority areas and Seebohm', *Social Work Today*, 1· 6, 1970.

47 I. F. Shaw, 'Agency decentralisation : planning and assessment', *British Journal of Social Work*, 3· 2, 1973.

48 *Local Authority and Allied Personal Social Services*, Cmnd 3703, HMSO, 1968, chapters 5 and 15.

49 P. Townsend and D. Wedderburn, *The Aged in the Welfare State*, Bell, 1965.

11

Summing up
Howard Jones

Until recently most social workers believed their role in society to be quite clear: what they had to do was to help the socially deprived and the social misfits to find a place and a decent life for themselves within society. In other words, they were concerned with helping people to make a better adjustment to life as it is. Very rarely did they question whether the society to which their clients were being asked to accommodate themselves was good enough—whether it might not even be the person who was well-adjusted to it who needed help, to make him less satisfied—demanding improvements and changes in it, rather than meekly accepting that all the concessions had to be on his side. Classical textbooks often saw social reform as a function of the social worker, but it was always marginal reform, an improvement in the efficiency or the scale of provision made by society rather than anything which challenged its basic presuppositions.

The most important of these unquestioned axioms was that of the primary importance of individual responsibility. The individual was seen as largely responsible for his own situation in life. To change that situation called for a change in him, a change in his motivations, so that he became more enterprising, more ambitious, more hard-working and thrifty. And if in spite of all, the rest of us, represented by the state, had to step in to rescue him, we had to beware that in so doing we did not damage that vital sense of his own responsibility for his own behaviour, by causing him to look always to the state for a solution. So we had to ensure that any help we gave him was accompanied by some form of deterrent punishment. Although some social workers have begun to question these ideas they still dominate our social services.

Consequently in spite of all the protestations about the 'means test' being a 'needs test' solely concerned with matching needs to benefits, it tends to carry with it as a deterrent a stigma, about the

167

existence of which recipients, at any rate, have no doubt. And it deters even where we claim we want people to accept help. Most older and some younger would-be claimants, have learned only too well their social ABC about the necessity of independence for self-respect. It is hypocritical of us for instance, to regret that elderly people, who need and are entitled to Supplementary Benefits, do not claim them, if we maintain such a climate of disapproval for those who do. The same pessimistic assumptions about human nature lay behind the belief (expressed in the 'wage stop') that a man would not look for a job if he received more from, say, supplementary benefits than he did in wages while at work. Never mind if he and his family had been barely subsisting on starvation wages. The 'iron law' of personal responsibility required that he must not be better off as a result of his (culpable?) dependence on the state. Put concisely: if he and his family were starving before, they must starve now. Otherwise, heaven help us, he might be demoralised, and human beings generally, being sons of Adam with a clear racial memory of those happy, labour-free days in Eden, would soon all be corrupted by his example.

The deterrent philosophy of the penal system is only a more obvious expression of this kind of thinking as applied to deviants, though it sometimes has even more ludicrous consequences. Nothing was more tragically comic than some of the arguments raised against the proposals in the Wolfenden Report that private homosexual relations between consenting adults should no longer be punished. To listen to the various gloomy prognostications about the increase in homosexuality which was likely to ensue, one would have thought that none of us were really carnally interested in the opposite sex but only in our own, and that we needed the threat of punishment to keep us on the straight and narrow. And this quite apart from the oversimplification of human psychology implicit in crudely deterrent ideas of this kind.

At least social workers (or most of them) take a more sophisticated view than this. While the state seems to have learned very little since this punitive philosophy was first formulated in the principle of 'less eligibility', with the reform of the Poor Law at the beginning of the last century, social workers have had Freud to enlighten them. It is true that the purpose of psychoanalysis remained that of helping the individual to function more effectively within the existing framework of society. This was always the aim of the personal analysis, and it is interesting to see how, for instance, industrial consultants influenced by psychoanalysis, in the years after the war, saw the works committees and other forms of worker consultation which they stimulated, as being largely concerned with improving communication and mutual understanding between workers and employers, rather than with bringing about radical changes in industry through pressure from the newly enfranchised workers. However in social work this personal accommodation was to be brought about not by the hit-and-miss method of externally imposed punishment, but through an inner change, a better insight into 'reality', brought about by analytically-oriented treatment. This was the target aimed at in the fifties by the best-trained caseworkers, and adopted as the ideal by the rest of the profession.

Social work was, of course, different also in another way. The deterrent approach of the state is not only crude but also callous. Social workers reflected the other side of society's ambivalence towards its needier but more annoying members. Social workers were *for* their clients—the very word 'client' was coined to reflect the social worker's sense of his duty towards them. Maybe the grosser inequities of society might occasionally make him wonder if he was meeting his obligations to his clients in encouraging them to conform, but psychoanalysis proved equal to the challenge. Just as the analyst 'treated' his patients and claimed a cure if the latter's aberrant behaviour ceased, so did the caseworker begin also to speak about his work with clients as 'treatment', and set as his aim the client's social health, as reflected in his acceptance of 'reality'. As I have pointed out elsewhere, the 'sickness hypothesis' enabled the social worker to satisfy at one and the same time the demand for personal responsibility and conformity, and also the obligation of the social worker towards his client. In helping him to conform, the social worker was curing him of a social malaise, and thus acting in his best interests.

What we have of course been witnessing in the evolution of professional social work has been the gradual scientisation and humanisation of the basic ideology of capitalism. In the nineteenth century, holding criminals and the poor responsible for their predicament was an expression of the universally applied protestant ethic, popularised by Samuel Smiles, and seen as the very mainspring of an enterprising and buoyant economy. Personal responsibility then speedily became an 'ethic' because, once we came to believe it to be a necessity, we rapidly made a virtue out of it. As its cruel consequences became apparent, compassionate persons sought to soften its impact for particular individuals by operating on the principle that the collision and therefore the damage is likely to be less if, in the face of the irresistible force, the immovable object can be made more tractable. Freud (himself a child of nineteenth-century individualism) provided the means.

Throughout the last thirty to forty years then, during which professional social work has been evolving, it has been nurtured by these certainties. It has known that it had an obligation to clients, which it could meet best by helping them to cope with their problems, and if possible, to change their attitudes so that they became more able to cope without social work help in the future, i.e. able to accept more responsibility for themselves. Changing society itself was for social workers clearly politics and not social work. The development of more reformist attitudes has not been assisted by the growth of the welfare state which has placed more and more social welfare activities in the hands of central or local government. The latter's elected members see democracy as requiring that they make the policy decisions while their staff, the social workers, carry them out. This places social workers who wish to argue for a change in the policies of their employing bodies, in a very weak position.

Nevertheless the scene is changing. After a few timid early alarums, the first real call to arms came with the publication of Barbara Wootton's book *Social Science and Social Pathology* fourteen years ago. Although she did less than justice to the skill and humane motivations of the caseworkers, she did social work the not inconsiderable service of calling attention to the root of many social problems in sheer inequality and social injustice. Professional social workers were enraged when she criticised what she saw as the pretentiousness, and the intrusion on privacy implicit in the intensive casework model, and called for the social worker to set his sights lower, becoming instead a kind of 'secretary' who would help the deprived to obtain their rights from the public social services. Theirs was a natural reaction, but like Lady Wootton's polemic, it was one-sided. She had revealed a 'blind spot' in their professional thinking as far as the structural aspects of social problems are concerned, and was entitled to ask them also if the psychological interplay between them and their clients was as egalitarian and free of suasion as they liked to believe.

As the contributions to this book show, these questions are now being raised by social workers as well as by outsiders like Wootton. In other words the era of certainty is past. Social workers are beginning to ask themselves not only what is the function of social work at the present: 'What social purpose are we colluding in?'; but also what ought its function to be: 'What social purpose should we be trying to achieve through the use of our professional skills?'

Mr Cypher in his pilot survey of members of the British Association of Social Workers shows that the 'activists', though a minority, are a force to be reckoned with in the profession. Their very 'activism' means that they probably exercise an influence out of proportion to their numbers. Moreover it would be a brave man who would say that the other categories of the 'therapists', 'traditionalists', and 'reformists' were uninfluenced by social reform ideas. Both he and Mr Mungham ascribe this change of attitude to certain structural changes in the work-setting and social characteristics of social workers, an increase in the number of men and of sociology graduates, changes in the organisation of the social services, and so on. No doubt these have played their part, though one cannot help but see the new militant radicalism in social work in the context of many manifestations of this kind in other areas of our society in recent years.

Students, and even schoolchildren, are much more militant about social injustice than they used to be, as are trade unions and even the CBI. It was a right-wing British government with its Family Income Supplement which broke with the sacred belief, extant ever since the beginning of the nineteenth century, that paying relief to people in full-time employment could only result in their moral deterioration. And although the government have often fallen from grace by their use of the stigmatising means-test, the new 'tax credit' income-tax system (a form of negative income tax) may eliminate its worst features by making it universal. So perhaps we are in the midst of one of those major shifts of opinion which occur only once in a hundred years or so. Just as competitive capitalism needed an individualist creed, so perhaps the growing collectivism and mutual interdependence of the present time is finding its own gospel. Not that the social sciences can be entirely exonerated. If nothing else, they have demonstrated to us the basic fallacy of extreme individualism, showing in contrast how very dependent we all are on one another; as well as the social origins of most of our social problems, making it impossible any longer for us to go on imputing the blame to the sufferers themselves.

It is in the controversies which surround the issue of Welfare Rights that the clash between the traditional and new-style 'activist' social worker is most obvious. Giving 'material aid' always had a rather pejorative ring to it in the minds of caseworkers. It was seen (as it had been by the Charity Organisation Society, a hundred years ago) as a potentially demoralising thing, to be used with an easy conscience only as an accessory in the primary task of changing the client's attitudes—so that he became more able to manage 'off his own bat' (i.e. without 'material aid') in the future. The emphasis as usual was being placed on personal responsibility rather than mutual interdependence. There does seem to have been a shift from such individualism in our thinking. Some reference has already been made to evidence of this in both public opinion and official policies. For instance, it is no longer possible to argue that retirement pensions are some sort of benevolent gift from the community to old people; it is widely agreed that after a lifetime of work, building up our culture and capital stock they have a *right* to a reasonable standard of comfort when they retire. Similarly, in a world in which unemployment is usually the result of the way in which our economic system operates, and is in no way the fault of the unemployed person himself, it is difficult to deny the latter's right to adequate maintenance. It should be emphasised that it is not merely the malfunctioning of the economic system which leads to unemployment. Economists are continually reminding us that the economy needs a certain level of unemployment in order to operate properly. We may feel justified in throwing people on to the industrial scrap-heap in the general interest, but surely not in insisting that they and their families shall then pay the price for it.

These are the kinds of issues which are brought into focus in Dr Walton's contribution to this book. If we still think in conventional terms it may seem astonishing to us that those who receive benefits or assistance from the public services should no longer be humbly grateful, but like latter-day Oliver Twists, demand even more. The very idea of a Claimants' Union still provokes something like apoplexy in many members of the public and quite a few social workers. But the idea of the 'right to welfare' is gaining ground steadily, and social workers as a result have to rethink their basic positions in the debate about individualism and collectivism.

To come out on the side of collectivism will probably often mean that social workers will have to become involved in militant activity with a definite political flavour, and (as already indicated) this presents problems, both for the social workers themselves and for their employers, where they are employed by the government or a local authority. It is not going to be easy for councillors to see their own social work employees carrying on a campaign against a policy instituted by the council, nor is it easy to justify such action. Dr Walton has begun to explore for us some of the ways in which this dilemma might be resolved. If it is not tackled it is going to be the cause of continuous friction and misunderstanding between social workers and their employing agencies, with incalculable effects upon their future relationship, as well as making it difficult for the politically active sections of the public to know who to hold to account and how to make their control effective. A less often recognised problem is that of giving the clients themselves some say; whatever the outcome of a power struggle between social workers and elected representatives, it will do little to give them any control over decisions which do, after all, affect them more than anybody else. Let us hope with Dr Walton that many social workers will recognise the need for client participation, and give support therefore to the right of representation of bodies like PROP and the Claimants' Union.

The problem of political accountability has, however, deeper roots than this. No matter how much they may regret and struggle against it, social workers (as Mr Fowler points out in his chapter) are, as things stand at present, going to remain part of the machinery of social control. They are concerned with transmitting currently dominant social values to their clients in the interest of social integration. Why else should dominant groups within society be willing to sanction the financing and support of social work? Social workers may perform other incidental functions, such as those of relieving suffering or humanising the social services, but always at present within a value context in which the individual's personal responsibility for 'fitting in' is taken for granted. The values to be transmitted may conceivably, as already suggested, be transforming themselves, and with them the broad objectives of social work, laying in the future perhaps less stress on the degrading effect of mutual dependence and personal gratification. Nevertheless, if we cannot find some other way of legitimating social choices than our present representative political system, social workers will continue in the last analysis to be as much the servants of the new establishment as they had been of the old. Irrespective of the outcome of all the battles (between dissenting social workers and local councils) the war will be lost, unless some fundamental rethinking on the nature of political organisation is undertaken. And social workers have more reason to turn their attention to this than most.

Meanwhile, here we are in 'no man's land'. A distinguished past, certainly. A future? Maybe. But our comforting certainty has gone. In the past, some of us had perhaps hoped that social research would provide us with a clear and unambiguous guide as to where the truth lay. There is still much to be hoped for from research. Mr Shaw in his essay has stripped away the rationalisations which social workers often used to protect them from the merciless onslaught of the researcher. They are not, for instance, as they have argued so often, dealing with unique cases in a uniquely individual fashion, but applying crude rules of thumb, based on unanalysed previous experience. At least the researcher takes care to ensure that the sample he studies is as representative as possible, and one therefore from which it is proper to draw generalisations. And he bases those generalisations on the laws of probability, after carefully counting the occurrences under investigation, rather than on fallible and uncounted recollections. But a clear and unambiguous guide? Statistics, as Mr Shaw sees, can never give us that in a land in which values, ideas about 'good and bad', 'right and wrong', are king.

Indeed some developments in the social sciences (notably what is

called 'phenomenological sociology') have compounded our uncertainties by suggesting that there are as many truths as there are
personal standpoints in relation to an issue. To the delinquent child,
his committal to an approved school is far from being the 'great
opportunity' which it is often seen to be by the juvenile court
which sends him there. We are back by another route at the point
already made about how to bring together the perceptions of
clients, social workers and elected representatives—and perhaps
more important, how to ensure that all have a share in the final
decision. As we have seen, this will call for changes in the political
field, but also, if social work is to remain (or become) a profession,
guided by a defensible moral conception of its role in the world,
these various warring claims will have somehow to be encompassed
within the network of ethical obligations which it is prepared to
meet. Mr Pearson wonders if the implications of this for social
work may not prove 'too hot to handle'. Let us hope not, for we
cannot camp out for ever in 'no man's land'.

Those who train social workers have a special responsibility here.
Perhaps in the past, practising social workers have been too ready
to leave all the theorising to the academics, and there is certainly
here a professional obligation on all social workers so compelling
that they cannot possibly be allowed to evade it any longer. All
the same, the school of social work, in training the social workers
of the future, does play an important part in determining what, for
social work, that future is going to be. Mr Deacon and Miss Bartley
describe a tradition in social work training, centred on psychoanalysis and individual attitudes rather than sociology and social
reform, which is still very powerful. As Mr Mungham points out,
it is a tradition which is slowly changing. Meanwhile the unresolved
disagreements remain and while they enliven discussion in senior
common rooms, they also oblige the students to 'make out' in one
practical situation after another, because of their consequent lack
of direction and of a firm identity. 'Opportunist social work' does
seem a contradiction in terms, and it would probably result in
mutual frustration for all concerned, but it might well be the end-
product of an educational process which makes it so difficult for
students to acquire a clear professional self-image. It is Mr Pearson's
problem once again : how to articulate a structure of professional
aims and ethics out of the present confusion. Reconciliation is one
conceivable solution, but the acceptance and institutionalisation of
difference may be more realistic, where one is dealing as here with
strong personal convictions, not therefore easily jettisoned.

The chapters by Professor Epstein and Mr Priestley examine two
of these contenders for the soul of social work. In spite of superficial
dissimilarities between them these two schools of thought are really

disputing with each other a single, possibly now tediously familiar question: should the individual be treated as a responsible being, with the right and duty to be involved in the shaping of his own future? It is easy enough to discern the assertion of a notion of individual responsibility in the 'New Careers' movement, and its denial in the determination of the behaviour therapist.

Yet it appears here in a new guise, demonstrating just how much vitality it has. For as Epstein and Priestley show, it can be seen not merely as a justification for blaming people, but as a rationale for the preservation of their rights and their self-determination. All of which demonstrates once again the difficulty of reaching a new consensus in social work rather than a constructive dialectic.

Professor Epstein is most concerned about the political implications of a psychology and a social work which sees nothing wrong in conditioning individuals mechanically into conformity. This danger is serious enough, but other issues also arise. To change an individual's behaviour independently of his own volition is probably a change which is not worth having. To be worth while it must arise from a change in the person's convictions. This is how society progresses morally, and not by an unthinking modification of our muscular contractions.

If behaviour therapy minimises participation, the 'New Careers' approach seeks to maximise it. The reform of individuals and society is no longer to be the exclusive preserve of professionals, but to be shared with a new kind of social worker who would be drawn from deprived and deviant groups themselves. They will know 'where the shoe pinches', and also ensure a share in the considerable power wielded by the social services, for the otherwise disfranchised people they represent. There is of course another side to 'New Careers', reflected in that name itself. One may have some misgivings, for example, about the use of ex-criminals for winning over their more incorrigible fellows, as a way of carving out new careers for themselves—the word 'quisling' comes too easily into one's mind. Nor is 'New Careers' as at present conceived, likely to present much of a threat to professional social work. Mr Priestley is very hostile (and many will feel provocative and rather unfair) in his comments on social workers, and yet wants his new careerists eventually to be able to join them.

There are many attractive features to 'New Careers'. If the 'indigenous non-professionals' (as they are sometimes called) can remain indigenous instead of becoming careerists then they have some chance of representing in the welfare process some other values than those of the 'haves'. And for the deprived to take a hand as a right in such matters, which are very much their affair, looks like a substantial improvement in the way we practise our conception of democracy. But what we are talking about here is how the clients and the claimants may be represented, not how to provide jobs for the more intelligent among them.

This is an aim which finds one form of expression in welfare rights groups, and some social workers have been able to identify themselves with these. Schools of social work, many social workers, and even the social services departments of some local authorities have paid lip service to the idea of community development, which by laying stress upon helping communities to define their own problems and decide for themselves how they should be solved, provides another way of achieving the power-sharing sought by 'New Careers'. The 'New Careers' idea of course envisages the clients penetrating further, even into social work practice itself. This whole trend towards client participation is perhaps the most significant of all in the confused social work scene at the present time, for it invokes most of our core problems—problems connected with the ethic of individualism, the distribution of power, the right to participate, and the right of dissent. Social workers cannot ignore it, and if they have understood the importance of replacing our present bogus uniformity by a more realistic acceptance of difference they will want to help it on.

For social work at the moment, then, there are no comforting certainties: but this means on the other hand that there is little likelihood of its subsiding into a rut. Society is changing before our eyes, and social workers have the opportunity of helping to reshape it. This is a rare privilege which will require some contribution from us—some hard thinking about the issues raised above, leading almost certainly to the sacrifice of some of our vested interests and of some of our professional shibboleths. We may also need the courage from time to time to stand up to established authority for the patterns of welfare and social work that we believe to be right. The nature of the challenge to us is clear. Are we as prepared as we expect our clients to be to face up to reality in this changing world? It could at least be an evolving rather than a static (and possibly decaying) reality and one which is emerging out of the views and aspirations of all sections of the community, rather than those of just a few.